CAMBRIDGE LIBRARY COLLECTION

Books of enduring scholarly value

Shakespeare and Renaissance Drama

Shakespeare, 450 years after his birth, ranks as one of the most frequently studied writers and dramatists in the English language. His works continue to fascinate audiences and readers. They have profoundly influenced world literature, and have been the subject of scholarly research ever since the seventeenth century. This series includes editions of the texts themselves, anthologies, and works by Shakespeare's contemporaries. It ranges from early literary criticism to imaginative forays into the lives of Shakespeare's characters (nineteenth-century precursors of fan fiction?), and also covers the historical context of Shakespeare's life and writings, and the actors who achieved fame in performing his plays.

An Essay on the Writings and Genius of Shakespear

The daughter of wealthy parents, and well educated in history and languages, at the age of twenty-one Elizabeth Robinson (1718–1800) married Edward Montagu, a grandson of the earl of Sandwich whose income derived from northern estates and coal-mines, and began to establish a London salon attended by the intellectual cream of British society, including Johnson, Burke, Garrick, and Hester Chapone. This 1778 work, written at the urging of her bluestocking friend Elizabeth Carter, is a spirited defence of Shakespeare from the criticism of Voltaire, comparing Shakespeare's genius to that of the ancient Greek and modern French poet-dramatists, and finding it superior. Voltaire is especially condemned in this lively and elegant piece for his efforts to measure Shakespeare against Corneille using an inadequate and mechanistic French translation of the English dramatist. Mrs Montagu's collected letters, and works by others of her circle, are also reissued in this series.

Cambridge University Press has long been a pioneer in the reissuing of out-of-print titles from its own backlist, producing digital reprints of books that are still sought after by scholars and students but could not be reprinted economically using traditional technology. The Cambridge Library Collection extends this activity to a wider range of books which are still of importance to researchers and professionals, either for the source material they contain, or as landmarks in the history of their academic discipline.

Drawing from the world-renowned collections in the Cambridge University Library and other partner libraries, and guided by the advice of experts in each subject area, Cambridge University Press is using state-of-the-art scanning machines in its own Printing House to capture the content of each book selected for inclusion. The files are processed to give a consistently clear, crisp image, and the books finished to the high quality standard for which the Press is recognised around the world. The latest print-on-demand technology ensures that the books will remain available indefinitely, and that orders for single or multiple copies can quickly be supplied.

The Cambridge Library Collection brings back to life books of enduring scholarly value (including out-of-copyright works originally issued by other publishers) across a wide range of disciplines in the humanities and social sciences and in science and technology.

An Essay on the Writings and Genius of Shakespear

Compared with the Greek and French Dramatic Poets:
With Some Remarks upon the Misrepresentations of
Monsieur de Voltaire

ELIZABETH MONTAGU

CAMBRIDGE
UNIVERSITY PRESS

CAMBRIDGE
UNIVERSITY PRESS

University Printing House, Cambridge, CB2 8BS, United Kingdom

Cambridge University Press is part of the University of Cambridge.
It furthers the University's mission by disseminating knowledge in the pursuit of
education, learning and research at the highest international levels of excellence.

www.cambridge.org
Information on this title: www.cambridge.org/9781108083911

© in this compilation Cambridge University Press 2018

This edition first published 1778
This digitally printed version 2018

ISBN 978-1-108-08391-1 Paperback

AN

ESSAY

ON THE

WRITINGS AND GENIUS

OF

SHAKESPEAR.

A N

E   S   S   A   Y

ON THE

WRITINGS AND GENIUS

OF

SHAKESPEAR,

COMPARED WITH THE

GREEK AND FRENCH DRAMATIC POETS,

WITH

SOME REMARKS

Upon the MISREPRESENTATIONS of

Monf. de VOLTAIRE.

DUBLIN:

Printed for J. POTTS, W. SLEATER, D. CHAM-
BERLAINE, J. WILLIAMS, and W. COLLES.

M,DCC,LXXVIII.

CONTENTS.

INTRODUCTION.

MR. Pope, in the preface of his edition of Shakefpear, fets out by declaring, that of all Englifh poets, this tragedian offers the fulleft and faireft fubject for criticifm. Animated by an opinion of fuch authority, fome of the moft learned and ingenious of our critics have made correct editions of his works, and enriched them with notes. The fuperiority of talents and learning, which I acknowledge in thefe editors leaves me no room to entertain the vain prefumption of attempting to correct any paffages of this celebrated author; but the whole, as corrected and elucidated by them, lies open to a thorough enquiry into the genius of our great Englifh claffic. Unprejudiced and candid judgment will be the fureft bafis of his fame. He is now in danger of incurring the fate of the heroes of the fabulous ages, on whom the vanity of their country, and the fuperftition of the times, beftowed an apotheofis founded on pretenfions to achievements beyond human capacity, by which they loft

in

in a more fceptical and critical age, the
glory that was due to them for what they
had really done ; and all the veneration
they had obtained, was afcribed to ignorant credulity, and national prepoffeffion.——
Our Shakefpear, whofe very faults pafs
here unqueftioned, or are perhaps confecrated through the enthufiafm of his admirers, and the veneration paid to long-
eftablifhed fame, is by a great wit, a great
critic, and a great poet of a neighbouring
nation, treated as the writer of monftrous
farces, called by him tragedies ; and barbarifm and ignorance are attributed to the
nation by which he is admired. Yet if
wits, poets, critics, could ever be charged with prefumption, one might fay there
was fome degree of it in pronouncing,
that in a country where Sophocles and Euripides are as well underftood as in any in
Europe, the perfections of dramatic poetry
fhould be as little comprehended as among
the Chinefe.

Learning here is not confined to ecclefi-
aftics, or a few lettered fages and acade-
mics ; every Englifh gentleman has an education, which gives him an early acquaintance with the writings of the ancients.
His knoweledge of polite literature dos not
begin

begin with the period which Mr. de Voltaire calls Le Siecle de Louis quatorze. Before he is admitted as a spectator at the theatre at London, it is probable he has heard the tragic muse as she spoke at Athens, and as she now speaks at Paris, or in Italy; and he can discern between the natural language in which she addressed the human heart, and the artificial dialect which she has acquired from the prejudices of a particular nation, or the jargon caught from the tone of a court. To please upon the French stage, every person of every age and nation was made to adopt their manners.

The heroes of antiquity were not more disguised in the romances of Calprenade and Scuderi than in the tragedies of Corneille. In spite of the admonition given by that admirable critic Boileau to their dramatic writers in the following lines:

Gardez donc de donner, ainsi que dans Clélie,
L'air ni l'esprit François à l'antique Italie;
Et sous des noms Romains faissant notre portrait,
Peindre Caton galant, & Brutus damoret.

The Horatii are represented no less obsequious in their address to their king than the courtiers of the grand monarque. Theseus

feus

feus is made a mere fighing fwain. Many
of the greateft men of antiquity, and even
the rougheft heroes among the Goths and
Vandals, were exhibited in this effeminate
form.   The poet dignified the piece, perhaps with the name of an Hercules, but,
alas! it was always Hercules fpinning that
was fhewn to the fpectator.   The editor
of Corneille's works, in terms fo grofs as
are hardly pardonable in fuch a mafter of
fine raillery, frequently attacks our Shakefpear for the want of politenefs in his
pieces : it muft be owned, that in fome
places they bear the marks of the unpolifhed times in which he wrote, but one
cannot forbear fmiling to hear a critic, who
profeffes himfelf an admirer of the tragedies of Corneille, object to the barbarifm
of Shakefpear's.   There never was a more
barbarous mode of writing than that of
the French Romances in the laft age, nor
which from its tedioufnefs, languor, and
want of truth of character is lefs fit to be
copied on the ftage : and what are moft of
the parts of Corneille's boafted tragedies,
but the romantic dialogue, its tedious foliloquy, and its extravagant fentiments in
the true Gothic livery of rhyme ?

The

The French poets aſſume a ſuperiority over Shakeſpear, on account of their more conſtant adherence to Ariſtotle's unities of time and place.

The pedant who bought at a great price the lamp of a famous philoſopher, expect-ing that by its aſſiſtance his lucubrations would become equally celebrated, was lit-tle more abſurd than thoſe poets who ſup-poſe their dramas will be excellent if they are regulated by Ariſtotle's clock. To bring within a limited time and an aſſigned ſpace certain ſeries of converſations (and French plays are little more) is no difficult matter; for that is the eaſieſt part of eve-ry art perhaps, but in poetry without diſ-pute, in which the connoiſſeur can direct the artiſt.

I do not believe the critic imagined that a mere obedience to his laws of drama would make a good tragedy, tho' it might prevent a poet more bold and judicious, from writing a very abſurd one. A pain-ter can define the juſt proportion of the human body, and the anatomiſt knows what muſcles conſtitute the ſtreng h of the limbs; but grace of motion and exertion of ſtrength, depend on the mind, which

animates

animates the form.   The critic but fafhi-
ons the body of a work ; the poet muft
add the foul, which gives force and direc-
tion to its actions, and geftures : when one
of thefe critics has attempted to finifh a
work by his own rules, he has rarely been
able to convey into it one fpark of divine
fire ; and the hero of his piece, whom he
defigned for a man, remains a cold inanimate ftatue ; which moving on the wood
and wire of the great mafters in the me-
chanical part of the drama, prefents to the
fpectators a kind of heroic puppet-fhew.
As thefe pieces take their rife in the fchool
of criticifm, they return thither again, and
are as good fubjects for the ftudents in that
art, as a dead body to the profeffors in
phyfic. Moft minutely too have they been
anatomifed in learned academies : but
works animated by genius will not abide
this kind of diffection.

Mr. Pope fays, that to form a judgment
of Shakefpear's works, we are not to apply to the rules of Ariftotle, which would be
like trying a man by the laws of one country, who lived under thofe of another.——
Heaven-born genius acts from fomething
fuperior to rules, and antecedent to rules ;
and has a right to appeal to nature herfelf.
                                        Great

Great indulgence is due to the errors of
original writers, who quitting the beaten
track which others have travelled, make
daring incurſions into unexplored regions of invention, and boldly ſtrike into
the pathleſs ſublime : it is no wonder if
they are often bwildered, ſometimes be-
nighted ; yet ſurely it is more eligible to
partake the pleaſure and the toil of their
adventures, than ſtill to follow the cautious ſteps of timid imitators/through trite
and common roads. Genius is of a bold
enterprizing nature, ill adapted to the
formal reſtraints of critic inſtitutions, or
indeed to lay down to itſelf rules of nice
diſcretion. If perfect and faultleſs compoſition is ever to be expected from human
faculties, it muſt be at ſome happy period
when a noble and graceful ſimplicity, the
reſult of well regulated and ſober magnanimity, reigns through the general manners.
Then the muſes and the arts, neither ef-
feminately delicate nor audaciouſly bold,
aſſume their higheſt character, and in all
their compoſitions ſeem to reſpect the chaſ-
tity of the public taſte, which would equally diſdain quaintneſs of ornament, or the
rude neglect of elegance and decorum.
Such periods had Greece, had Rome! Then
were produced immortal works of every

kind!

kind! But, when the living manners dege-
nerated, in vain did an Ariſtotle and a Quin-
tilian endeavour to reſtore by doctrine
what had been inſpired by ſentiments, and
faſhioned by manners.

If the ſeverer muſes, whoſe ſphere is the
library and the ſenate, are obliged in complaiſance to this degeneracy, to trick themſelves out with meretricious and frivolous
ornaments, as is too apparent from the
compoſitions of the hiſtorians and orators
in declining empires, can we wonder that
a dramatic poet, whoſe chief intereſt it is
to pleaſe the people, ſhould, more than any
other writer, conform himſelf to their humour ; and appear moſt ſtrongly infected
with the faults of the times, whether they
be ſuch as belong to unpoliſhed, or corrupted taſte.

Shakeſpear wrote at a time when learning was tinctured with pedantry : wit was
unpoliſhed, and mirth ill-bred. The court
of Elizabeth ſpoke a ſcientific jargon, and
a certain obſcurity of ſtyle was univerſally
affected. James brought an addition of
pedantry, accompanied by indecent and
indelicate manners and language. By con-
tagion, or from complaiſance to the taſte of
the

the public, Shakefpear falls fometimes into the fafhionable mode of writing : but
this is only by fits ; for many parts of all
his plays are written with the moft noble,
elegant, and uncorrupted fimplicity. Such
is his merit, that the more juft and refined
the tafte of the nation has become, the
more he has encreafed in reputation. He
was approved by his own age, admired by
the next, and is revered and almoft adored
by the prefent. His merit is difput d by
little wits, and his errors are the jefts of little critics ; but there has not been a great
poet, or great critic, fince his time, who
has not fpoken of him with the higheft
veneration, Mr. Voltaire excepted. His
tranflations often, his criticifms ftill often-
er, prove he did not perfectly underftand
the words of the author ; and therefore it
is certain he could not enter into his meaning. He comprehended enough to perceive
he was unobfervant of fome eftablifh d rules
of compofition ; the facility with which he
performs what no rules can teach efcapes
him.   Will not an intelligent fpectator admire the prodigious ftructures of Stone-
Henge, becaufe he does not know by what
law of mechanics they were raifed ? Like
them, our author's works will remain for
ever the greateft monuments of the amaz-

ing force of nature, which we ought to
view as we do other prodigies, with an
attention to, and admiration of their ſtu-
pendous parts, and proud irregularity of
greatneſs.

It has been already declared that Shakeſpear is not to be tried by any code of critic laws ; nor is it more equitable to judge
him entirely by the practice of any particular theatre. Yet ſome criterion muſt be
eſtabliſhed by which we may determine his
merits. Firſt, we muſt take into conſideration what is propoſed to be done by the
means of dramatic imitation. Every ſpecies of poetry has its diſtinct offices. The
effecting certain moral purpoſes, by the
repreſentation of a fable, ſeem to have been
the univerſal intention, from the firſt inſti-
tution of the drama to this time ; and to
have prevailed, not only in Europe, but in
all countries where the dramatic art has
been attempted. It has indeed been the
common aim of all poetry to pleaſe and in-
ſtruct ; but by means as various as the
kinds of compoſition. We are pleaſed with
the ode, the elegy, the eclogue ; not only
for having invention, ſpirit, elegance, and
ſuch perfections as are neceſſary to recom-
mend any ſort of poetry, but we alſo require

quire that each fhould have its fpecific merit ; the ode, that which conftitutes the
perfection of an ode, &c. In thefe views,
then, our author is to be examined. Fi.ft,
if his fables anfwer the nobleft end of fable, moral inftruction ; next, whether his
dramatic imitation has its proper dramatic
excellence.   In the latter of thefe articles,
perhaps, there is not any thing will more
affift our judgment than a candid comparifon (wh re the nature of the fubject will
bear it) between his and fome other celebrated dramatic compofitions.   It is idle
to refer to a vague, unrealized idea of perfection : we may fafely pronounce that to
be well executed, in any art, which after
the repeated efforts of great geniufes is e-
qual to any thing that has been produced
We may fecurely applaud what the ancients have crowned ; therefore fhould not
withold our approbation wherever we find
our countryman has equalled the moft admired paffages in the Greek tragedians :-
but we fhall not do juftice to his native talents, when they are the object of confideration, if we do not remember the different
circumftances under which thefe writings
were compofed.   Shakefpear's plays were
to be acted in a paltry tavern, to an unlettered audience, juft emerging from barbarity :

rity : the Greek tragedies were to be exhibited at the public charge, under the
care and aufpices of the magiftrates at
Athens; where the very populace were critics in wit, and connoiffeurs in public
fpectacles. The period when Sophocles
and Euripides wrote, was that in which
the fine arts, and polite literature, were
in a degree of perfection which fucceeding
ages have emulated in vain.

It happened in the literary as in the moral world ; a few fages, from the veneration
which they had obtained by extraordinary wifdom and a faultlefs conduct, rofe to
the authority of legiflators. The practice
and manner of the three celebrated Greek
tragedians were by fucceeding critics eftablifhed as dramatic laws : happily for
Shakefpear, Mr. Johnfon, whofe genius
and learning render him fuperior to a fer·
vile awe of pedantic inftitutions, in his ingenious preface to his edition of Shakefpear has greatly obviated all that can be
objected to our author's neglect of the unities of time and place.

Shakefpear's felicity has been rendered
compleat in his age. His genius produced
works that time could not deftroy   but
fome

fome of the lighter characters were become illegible; thefe have been reftored by critics whofe learning and penetration traced back the veftiges of fuperannuated opinions and cuftoms. They are now no longer in danger of being effaced, and the teftimonies of thefe learned commentators to his merit, will guard our author's great monument of human wit from the prefumptuous invafions of our rafh critics, and the fquibs of our witlings; fo that the bays will flourifh unwithered and inviolate round his tomb; and his very fpirit feems to come forth and to animate his characters, as often as Mr. Garrick, who acts with the fame infpiration with which he wrote, affumes them on the ftage.

After our poet had received fuch important fervices from the united efforts of talents and learning in his behalf, fome apology feems neceffary for this work. Let it be remembered that the moft fuperb and lafting monument that ever was confecrated to beauty, was that to which every lover carried a tribute. I dare hope to do him honour only by augmenting the heap of volumes given by his admirers to his memory; I will own I was incited to this undertaking by great admiration of his genius

nius, and ftill greater indignation at the
treatment he had received from a French
wit, who feems to think he has made prodigious conceffions to our prejudices in favour of the works of our countryman in al-
lowing them the credit of a few fplendid paffages, while he fpeaks of every entire piece
as a monftrous and ill-conftructed farce. —
Ridiculoufly has our poet, and ridiculoufly
has our tafte been reprefented, by a writer
of univerfal fame ; and through the medi-
um of an almoft univerfal language. Su-
perficial criticifms hit the level of fhallow
minds, to whom a bon mot will ever appear reafon, and an epigrammatic turn argument; fo that many of our countrymen
have haftily adopted this lively writer's
opinion of the extravagance and total want
of defign in Shakefpear's dramas. With
the more learned, deep, and fober critics
he lies under one confiderable difadvantage.
For copying nature as he found it in the
bufy walks of human life, he drew from
an origina , with which the literati are feldom well acquainted. They perceive his
portraits are not of the Grecian or of the
Roman fchool : after finding them unlike
to the celebrated forms preferved in learned mufeums they do not deign to enquire
whether they refemble the living perfons
　　　　　　　　　　　　　　　they

they were intended to reprefent. Among thefe connoiffeurs, whofe acquaintance with the characters of men is formed in the library, not in the ftreet, the camp, or village, whatever is unpolifhed and uncouth paffes for fantaftic and abfurd, though, in fact, it is a faithful reprefentation of a really exifting character.

But it muft be acknowledged, that, when this objection is obviated there will yet remain another caufe of cenfure; for though our author, from want of delicacy or from a defire to pleafe the popular tafte, thought he had done well when he had faithfully copied nature, or reprefented cuftoms, it will appear to politer times the error of an untutored mind; which the example of judicious artifts, and the admonitions of delicate-connoiffeurs had not taught, that only graceful nature and decent cuftoms give proper fubjects for imitation It may be faid in mitigation of his fault that the vulgar here had not, as at Athens, been ufed to behold,

> Gorgeous tragedy
> In fcepter'd pall come fweeping by,
> Prefenting Thebes or Pelops' line,
> Or the tale of Troy divine.

Homer's

Homer s works alone were fufficient to teach the Greek poets how to write, and their audience how to judge. The fongs fung by our bards at feafts and merry-makings were of a very coarfe kind : As the people were totally illiterate, and only the better fort could read even their mother tongue, their tafte was formed on thefe compofitions. As yet our ftage had exhibited only thofe palpable allegories by which rude unlettered moralifts inftruct and pleafe the grofs and ignorant multitude. Nothing can more plainly evince the opinion the poets of thofe times had of the ignorance of the people, than the condefcenfion fhewn to it by the learned Earl of Dorfet in his tragedy of Gorboduc ; in which the moral of each act is reprefented on the ftage in dumb fhew. It is ftrange that Mr. de Voltaire who affects an impartial and philofophic fpirit, fhould not rather fpeak with admiration than contempt of an author, who by the force of genius rofe fo much above the age and circumftances in which he was born, and who, even when he deviates moft from rules, *can rife to faults true critics dare not mend.* In delineating characters he muft be allowed far to furpafs all dramatic writers, and even Homer himfelf ; he gives an air of reality
to

to every thing, and in fpite of many and great faults, effects, better than any one has done, the chief purpofes of the theatrical reprefentation. It avails little to prove that the means by which he effects them are not thofe prefcribed in any art of poetry. While we feel the power and energy of his predominant genius, fhall we not be apt to treat the cold formal precepts of the critic, with the fame peevifh contempt that the good lady in the Guardian, fmarting in the anguifh of a burn, does her fon's pedantic intrufion of Mr. Lock's doctrine, to prove that there is no heat in fire. Nature and fentiment will pronounce our Shakefpear to be a mighty genius; judgment and tafte will confefs that as a writer he is far from being faultlefs.

ON

DRAMATIC POETRY.

O N

DRAMATIC POETRY.

TO form a true judgment of the merit cf any dramatic compofition, we ſhould firſt conſider the offices and ends of the drama; what are its pretenſions, and for what purpoſes it aſſumes a manner ſo different from any other kind of poetical imitation. The epic poem and the trage- dy, ſays Ariſtotle, are purely imitations *; but the dramatic is an imitation of the ac- tions of men, by the means of action itſelf. The epic is alſo an imitation of the actions of men, but it imitates by narration. The moſt perfect, and the beſt imitation, is cer- tainly that which gives the moſt adequate, lively, and faithful copy of the thing imi- tated. Homer was ſo ſerrſible of the ſupe- rior force and efficacy of the dramatic man- ner, that he often drops the narrative to aſ- ſume it; and Ariſtotle ſays, that for hav- ing invented the dramatic imitation, and not

* Ariſt. Poet. C. 1. Chap. 3.

not only on account of his other excellencies, He alone deferves the name of poet *

It is apparent, therefore, how far this
great critic prefers this, to every other fpecies of imitation.

The general object of poetry, among
the ancients, was the inftruction of mankind, in religion, morals, philofophy, &c.
To thefe great purpofes were tuned the
harps of Orpheus, Mufæus, Hefiod, Calli-
machus, &c. Nor in Greece alone was
poetry the teacher, and the guardian of
the fanctities of human fociety. † Our
Northern bards affumed the fame holy offices; the fame facred character. They directed the modes of divine worfhip: they
taught the moral duties; infpired and celebrated heroic deeds; fung the praifes of
valour, and the charms of liberty; and
fnatched from oblivion the bold achievements, and meritorious acts, of patriots,
and of heroes. In the Eaft, the poet veil-
ed his inventions in myft rious allegories
and divine mythology; and rather endeavoured to raife the mind to heavenly con-
templations, than to inftruct it in human
affairs.

* Chap. 4.   † Hiftoire des Celtes, l. 2. c. 9.

In

In Greece, the general mother of arts, arofe the mighty genius of Homer; of whom it may be faid, as it is of Socrates with relation to philofophy, that he brought poetry from heaven, to live in cities a- mong men. The moral of the fable of the Iliad is adapted to the political ftate of Greece, whofe various chiefs are hereby ex- horted to unanimity; the Odyffey, to the general condition of human nature; but the epifodical part of his works he has en- riched with mythology, phyfical allegory, the fine arts, and whatever adorned the mind of man, or bleft fociety; even rules of domeftic œconomy, focial behaviour, and all the fweet civilities of life, are taught by this great mafter, of what may be called, in the moft enlarged fenfe, the humanities. Yet firft in the rank of all the eminent perfections of this unequal- ed bard, is placed the invention of the dramatic imitation, by a critic, whofe judgment was formed by philofophy, and a deep knowledge of human nature. He faw the powerful agency of living words, joined to moving things, when ftill narra- tion yields the place to animated action.

It is as a moral philofopher, not as the mere connoiffeur in a polite art, that Ariftotle

totle gives the preference, above all other modes of poetic imitation, to tragedy, as capable to purge the paffions, by the means of pity and terror *. The object of the epic poem is to infpire magnanimity; to give good documents of life; to induce good habits ‡, and, as a wholefome regimen, to preferve the whole moral œconomy in a certain foundnefs and integrity. But it is not compofed of ingredients of fuch efficacy as to fubdue the violent diftempers of the mind, nor can apply its art to the benefit of the ignorant vulgar, where thofe diftempers are in their moft exafperated ftate. An epic poem is too abftrufe for the people; the moral is too much enveloped, the language too elevated for their apprehenfion; nor have they leifure, or application, to trace the confequences of ill-governed paffions, or erroneous principles, through the long feries of a voluminous work. The drama is happily conftituted for this purpofe. Events are brought within the compafs of a fhort period : precepts are delivered in the familiar way of difcourfe : the fiction is concealed, the allegory is realized : and reprefentation and action take the place of

* Chap. 6.   ‡ Du Poeme Epique par Boffu, l. 2. c. 17.

cold

cold unaffecting narration. A tragedy is
a fable exhibited to the view, and rendered palpable to the senses ; and every deco-
ration of the stage is contrived to impose
the delusion on the spectator, by conspir-
ing with the imitation. It is addressed to
the imagination, through which it opens
to itself a communication to the heart,
where it is to excite certain passions and
affections : each character being personat-
ed, and each event exhibited, the attention of the audience is greatly captivated,
and the imagination so far aids in the delusion, as to sympathize with the representation. To the muse of tragedy, therefore, Mr. Pope has assigned the noble task,

> To wake the soul by tender strokes of art,
> To raise the genius, and to mend the heart.
> To make mankind in conscious virtue bold,
> Live o'er each scene, and be what they behold.

He ascribes such power to a well-wrought
scene, as to ask,

> When Cato groans who does not wish to bleed?

He would not have supposed the death
of Hector, or Sarpedon, to have had an
equal effect on any reader of the Iliad ;
such enthusiasm is to be caught only from
the stage, and is the effect alone of strong-
working sympathy, and passions agitated

C   by

by the peculiar force and activity of the
dramatic manner. Writers of feeble genius, in their compofitions for the ftage,
frequently deviate into the narrative and
defcriptive ftyle; a fault for which nothing can atone; for the drama is a fpecies
of poetry, as diftinct from the epic, as
ftatuary from painting; and can no more
receive that merit which fpecifically belongs to it, and conftitutes its perfection,
from fine verfification, or any other poetical ornaments, than a ftatue can be rendered a fine fpecimen of fculpture, from
being beautifully coloured, or highly po-
lifhed. It is frivolous and idle therefore
to infift on any little incidental and accef-
fory beauties, where the main part, the
very conftitution of the thing is defective.
Yet on fome trivial beauties do the French
found all their protenfions to fuperiority
and excellence in the drama.

According to Ariftotle there can be no
tragedy without action   Mr. Voltaire
confeffes that fome of the moft admired
tragedies in France, are rather converfa-
tions, than reprefentations of an action.
It will hardly be allowed to thofe who fail

* Arift chap. vi.

in the moſt eſſential part of an art, to ſet
up their performances as models. Can they
who have robbed the tragic muſe of all her
virtue, and diveſted her of whatſoever
gave her a real intereſt in the human heart,
require we ſhould adore her for the glitter
of a few falſe brilliants, or the nice arange-
ment of frippery ornaments? If ſhe wears
any thing of intrinſic value it has been
borrowed from the ancients; but by theſe
artiſts it is ſo fantaſtically faſhioned to
modern modes, as to loſe all its original
graces, and even that neceſſary qualificati-
on of all ornament, fitneſs and propriety.
A French tragedy is a tiſſue of declamations, and ſome laboured recitals of the cataſtrophe, by which the ſpirit of the drama
is greatly weakened and enervated, and
the theatrical piece is deprived of that peculiar influence over the mind, which it
derives from the vivid force of repreſentation.

Segnius irritant animos demiſſa per aurem,
Quam quæ ſunt oculis ſubjecta fidelibus, et quæ
Ipe ſibi tradit ſpectator.

The buſineſs of the drama is to excite
ſympathy; and its effect on the ſpectator
depends on ſuch a juſtneſs of imitation, as
ſhall

ſhall cauſe, to a certain degree, the ſame
paſſions and affeētions, as if what is exhibited was real. We have obſerved narrative imitation to be too faint and feeble
a means to excite paſſion : declamation,
ſtill worſe, plays idly on the ſurface of the
ſubjeēt, and makes the poet, who ſhould
be concealed in the aētion, viſible to the
ſpeētator. In many works of art, our pleaſure ariſes from a refleētion on the art itſelf;
and in a compariſon, drawn by the mind,
between the original and the copy before
us. But here the art and the artiſt muſt
not appear ; for as often as we recur to
to the poet, ſo often our ſympathy with the
aētion on the ſtage is ſuſpended. The
pompous declamations of the French theatre are mere rhetorical flouriſhes, ſuch as
an unintereſted perſon might make on the
ſtate of the perſons in the drama. They
aſſume the office of the ſpeētator by ex-
preſſing his feelings, inſtead of conveying
to us the ſtrong emotions and ſenſations of
the perſons under the preſſure of diſtreſs.
Experience informs us, that even the inarticulate groans, and involuntary convul-
ſions, of a creature in agonies, affeēt us
much more than the moſt eloquent and
elaborate deſcription of its ſituation, delivered in the propereſt words, and moſt
                              ſignificant

fignificant geftures.   Our pity is attendant
on the paffion of the unhappy perfon and
on his own fenfe of his misfortunes.   From
defcription, from the report of a fpeƈtator,
we may make fome conjeƈture of his internal ftate of mind, and fo far we fhall be
moved : but the direƈt and immediate way
to the heart, is by the fufferer's expreffion
of his paffion.   As there may be fome obfcurity in what I have faid on this fubjeƈt,
I will endeavour to illuftrate the doƈtrine
by examples.

Sophocles, in his admirable tragedy of
Œdipus Coloneus, makes Œdipus expof-
tulate with his undutiful fon.   The injured parent expofes the enormity of filial difobedience ; fets forth the duties of this relation in a very ftrong and lively manner ;
but it is only by the vehemence with which
he fpeaks of them, and the imprecations
he utters againft the delinquent fon, that
we can guefs at the violence of the emotions ; therefore he excites more indignation at the conduƈt of Polynices, than fympathy with his own forrow ; of what we
can judge only as fpeƈtators ; for he has
explained to us merely the external duties
and relations of parent and child.   The
pangs of paternal tendernefs, thus wound-

ed, is more pathetically expreſſed by King
Lear, who leaves out whatever of this e-
normity is equally ſenſible to the ſpectator,
and immediately expoſes to us his own internal feelings, when, in the bitterneſs of
his ſoul, curſing his daughters offspring,
he adds,

> That ſhe may feel,
> How ſharper than a ſerpent's tooth it is,
> To have a thankleſs child.

By this we perceive how deeply paternal
affection is wounded by filial ingratitude.

In the play of King John, the legate offers many arguments of conſolation to
Conſtance, on the loſs of Arthur : they
appear, to the ſpectator, reaſonable, till
ſhe ſo ſtrongly expreſſes the peculiar ten-
terneſs of maternal love, by anſwering,

> He ſpeaks to me that never had a ſon.

One might be made to conceive, in ſome
degree, the horrors of a murderer, under
whoſe knife the bleeding victim is expiring
in agonies, by a deſcription of the unhappy object ; but how fully, and how forci-
bly, is the conſciouſneſs of guilt expreſſed
by Macbeth, when, ſpeaking of the grooms
who lay near Duncan, he ſays !

MACBETH.

MACBETH.

One cry'd, God blefs us! and Amen! the other ;
As they had feen me with thefe hangman's hands,
Liftening their fear.   I could not fay, Amen,
When they did fay, God blefs us !

Thefe expreffions open to us the internal ftate of the perfons interefted, and never fail to command our fympathy. Shakefpear feems to have had the art of the
Dervife, in the Arabian tales, who could
throw his foul into the body of another man,
and be at once poffeffed of his fentiments,
adopt his paffions, and rife to all the func-
tions and feelings of his fituation.

Shakefpear was born in a rank of life, in
which men indulge themfelves in a free expreffion of their paffions, with little regard
to exterior appearance. This perhaps made
him more acquainted with the movements
of the heart, and lefs knowing or obfervant
of outward forms : againft the one he often
offends, he very rarely mifreprefents the
other. The French tragedians, on the contrary, attend not to the nature of the man
whom they reprefent, but to the decorums
of his rank : fo that their beft tragedies are
made ridiculous, by changing the condition of the perfons of the drama; which
C 4   could

could not be fo eafily effected if they fpoke
the language of paffion, which in all ranks
of men is much alike. This kind of exterior reprefentation falls intirely fhort of
the intention of the drama ; and indeed
many plays are little more than poems re-
hearfed ; and the theatrical decorations are
ufed rather to improve the fpectacle, than
to affift the drama of which the poet remains the apparent hero. We are told by
a French critic, that the great pleafure of
their audience arifes from a reflection on
the difficulty of rhyming in that language.
—If that be the cafe, it is plain neither
the French tragedians endeavour at, or
their audience expect from them, the true
perfections of drama. For, by the fame
rule, if Hercules was reprefented under the
difficulties of performing any of the tafks
enjoined by Euryftheus, the attention of
the audience would not be engaged fo
much to the means by which he atchieved
his heroic labours, as to the fweat and toil
of the poet in his clofet, in afforting male
and female rhymes. We have already re-
marked, that the more we revert from the
ftage to the poet, the lefs we fhall be affected with what is acted ; and therefore
if the difficulty of rhyme, and its apparent difference from the common language
of

of dialogue, be fuch as continually to fet
the art and the artift before ourfelves, the
fpecific meric of a piece intended to conceal the poet, and reprefent certain perfons
and events, does not in any degree, ex ft in
fuch compofitions. Sophocles certainly unfolds the fatal myftery of the birth of
Œdipus with great art : but our intereft
in the play arifes not from reflection on
the conduct of the poet, but is the effect
of his making us alternately hope and fear
for this guiltlefs, unhappy man.   We wait
with trembling expectation for the anfwer
of the oracle, and for the teftimony of
Phorbas, becaufe we imagine that the deftiny of Oedipus, and the fate of Thebes,
depend on them : if we confidered it merely as the contrivance of the poet, we fhould
be as unconcerned at the unravelling of the
plot, as about the explication of a riddle.

The affectation of elaborate art is certainly among the falfe refinements of the
modern ftage.—The firft mafters in theatrical reprefentaitons made ufe of a diction,
which united the harmony of verfe to the
eafy and natural air of profe, and was fuited to the movement, and buftle of action,
being confidered only as fubfervient to the

C 5   fable.

fable, and not as the principal object of the poet or the audience.

The firſt endeavour of the poet ſhould be to touch the heart, and next to mend it. What would the ancients ſay, who would not ſuffer even the inarticulate ſounds of muſic, to utter tones that might enervate the mind, if they could hear the ſtage, from whence iſſued precepts that awakened the magiſtrate, animated the chief, and improved the citizen, now giving leſſons of love ; and the dramatic art, no longer attempting to purge the paſſions by pity and terror, but by falſe delicacy diveſted of its power, and diverted from its end, melting away in the ſtrains of elegy and eclogue ? May we not venture to affirm ſuch refinements to be rather abuſe and degeneracy. than advances towards perfection ? Theſe poets have plainly neglected the moral ends which were the object of the drama ; and the manner of conducting their tragedy ſeems no leſs a deviation from that which the great poets practiſed, and the beſt critics taught. If they have avoided monſtrous errors and abſurdities, it is but the common privilege of mediocrity to do ſo ; but let not mediocrity aſſume the airs and preſumption of excellence and perfection, nor pretend to obtrude on others, as rules,
any

any fantaftical forms w iich affectation of
fafhion may have impofed on them.

It cannot be denied, but there fhould be
fome complaifance to the change of manners and opinions. Our delicacy would be
juftly offended, if the loud groans and nau-
feous wounds of Philoctetes were imitated
on the ftage ; but would good fenfe be lefs
offended, if, in the conduct of the play,
his fierce refentment of his wrongs, the
noble franknefs of the fon of Achilles, and
the crafty wiles of Ulyffes, which are fo
finely exhibited in the tragedy of Sophocles, and fo deeply intereft us in the difpute for the arrows, were all neglected, in
order to engage our attention to fome love-
fcenes between Neoptolemus, and a fair
nymph of Lemnos? Would the poet be
excufed by pleading the effeminacy and
gallantry of an audience, who would not
endure fo unpleafing an object as a wounded man, nor attend to any conteft but a-
bout a heart? In fuch a country the lyre
fhould warble melting ftrains : but let not
example teach us to fetter the energy, and
enervate the nobler power of the Britifh
mufe, and of a language fit to exprefs fub-
limer fentiments. The bleeding, fightlefs
eyes of Œdipus are objects of too great
horror

horror for the fpectator; but is not Thefeus, in the midft of plagues and famine,
adoring les beaux yeux of the princefs
Dirce as much an object of ridicule?

Fine dialogues of love, interwoven with
a tale of inceft and murder, would not
have been indured in any country where
tafte had not been abfolutely perverted.
Mr. Voltaire has the candour to own this is
a bad tragedy; but Corneille tells us, it
was his good fortune to find it the general
opinion, that none of his pieces were compofed with more art: fo little was the dramatic art underftood in the polite court of
Louis XIV. The Œdipus of Corneille is
fo far below criticifm, that I fhould not
have taken any notice of it but as it was
neceffary to bring a ftrong proof of the de-
pravity of tafte in thofe times.

Mr. Voltaire has endeavoured to con-
vince his country men, that the metaphy-
fics, of love, and the fophiftry of politics,
are not adapted to the theatre: but he
durft not bring the ftory of Œdipus on
the ftage without fome love fcenes; and
Philoctetes, the companion of Hercules, is
introduced fighing for the autumnal
charms

charms of Jocaſta.——One may ſurely ſay
with her,

JOCASTA.
D'un lien charmant le ſoin tendre & timide
Ne dut point occuper le ſucceſſeur d'Alcide.

Tragedy, thus converted into mere amorous ditty, drops all the ends of her inſti-
tution, which were, ſays Sir P. Sydney †,
" to open the greateſt wounds, and to ſhew
" forth the ulcers that are covered with
" tiſſue; to make kings fear to be tyrants,
" tyrants to manifeſt their tyrannical hu-
" mours; that ſtirring the effects of admi-
" ration and commiſeration, teacheth the
" uncertainty of this world, and upon how
" weak foundations gilded roofs are build-
" ed; that maketh us know, qui ſceptra
" ſævus duro imperio regit, timet timen-
" tes, metus in autorem redit." The
example to the great; the warnings to the
people; all high and public precepts are
neglected; and by making the intereſt of
the play turn upon the paſſion of love, to
which the man, the prince, the hero, is
made to ſacrifice every other conſideration,
even private morals are corrupted. Of
this we ſhall be perfectly convinced, if we
compare the conduct and ſentiments of

† Defence of Poeſy.

Theſeus,

Thefeus, and of the unfortunate daughter of Jocafta, in Antigone, and Œdipus
Coloneus, with the Thefeus and Dirce of
Corneille; where the enamoured pair dif-
claim all other regards and duties, human
and divine, for the character of mere
lovers.   In this play, great violence is done
to the character of the perfons, to which
Horace, and all good critics prefcribe a
moft exact adherence.   And though the
Romans, who had conquered all other nations, had the beft right to prefer their
own manners, and defpife thofe of other
countries,   yet their critics inculcated the
neceffity of imitating thofe of the people
reprefented.

The French tragedians not only deviate
from the character of the individual reprefented, but even from the general character of the age and country.   Thefeus and
Achilles are not only unlike to Thefeus and
Achilles, but they are not Greeks. Sophocles and Euripides never introduce a hero
who had appeared in the Iliad or Odyffey,
without a ftrict attention to making him act
fuitably to the opinion conceived of him
from thofe epic poems. When Ulyffes, in
the tragedy of Hecuba, comes to demand
Polixena to be facrificed, how admirably
is

is his conduct fuited to our conceptions of
him : He is cold, prudent, deaf to pity,
blind to beauty, and to be moved only by
confideration of the public weal. See him
in the Iphigenia of Racine, on a fimilar occafion, where he tells Agamemnon, *he
is ready to cry,*

Je fuis pret de pleurer ;

and examine whether there appears any
thing of Ulyffes upon the ftage but his
name. Nor is there a greater refemblance
between the French and Greek Achilles.
Euripides paints him with a peculiar franknefs and warmth of character, abhorrent
of fraud, and highly provoked when he
difcovers his name has been ufed in a deceit.
When he fees Iphigenia preferring the
good of her country, and an immortal
fame to the pleafures of life, he is then
ftruck with fentiments fo fuitable to the
greatnefs of his own mind ; and, in the
ftyle of a hero and a Greek, expreffes how
glad he fhould have been of fuch a bride.
The Achilles of Racine is not diftinguifhed from any young lover of fpirit ; yet
this is one of the beft French tragedies.

It is ufual to compliment Corneille with
having added dignity to the Romans ; and
he has undoubtedly given them a certain
ftrained

ftrained elevation of fentiment and expreffion, which has perhaps a theatrical greatnefs; but this is not Roman dignity, nor
fuitable to the character of republicans;
for, as the excellent Bifhop of Cambray
obferves *, hiftory reprefents the Romans
great and high in fentiment, but fimple,
modeft, natural in words, and very unlike the bombaft, turgid heroes of romance.   A great man, fays he, does not
declaim like a comedian,. his expreffions
in converfation are juft and ftrong ; he
utters nothing low, nor any thing pompous.   Auguftus Cælar, reprefented to a
barbarous audience, would command more
refpect, if feated on the Mogul's golden
throne, fparkling with gems, than in the
curule chair, to which power, not pomp,
gave dignity.   It is a degree of barbarifm
to afcribe noblenefs of mind to arrogance
of phrafe, or infolence of manners.   There
is a certain expreffion of ftyle and behaviour which verges towards barbarifm; a
ftate to which we may approach by roads
that rife, as well as by thofe that fall.   An
European monarch would think it as unbecoming him to be ftyled light of the
world, glory of nations, and fuch other
fwelling additions, affumed by the Afiatic

* Lettres fur l'Eloquence, &c.

princes.

princes, as to be called the tamer of horfes,
or the fwift-footed, like the heroes of
Homer.

Pere Brumoy feems to be very fenfible
of Corneille's mifreprefentation of the Roman character, though he fpeaks of it in
all the ambiguity of language which prudence could fuggeft, to one who was
thwarting a national opinion †. He talks
of *un raffinement de fierté* in the Romans,
and afks, if they are of this globe, or fpirits of a fuperior world ? The Greeks of
Racine, fays he, are not indeed of that
univerfe which belonged only to Corneille;
but with what pleafure does he make us
behold ourfelves in the perfons he prefents
to us! and how agreeably would the heroes of antiquity be furprifed to find themfelves adorned by new manners, not indeed like their own, but which yet do not
mifbecome them !

It can hardly be fuppofed that a critic of
Pere Brumoy's tafte did not mean to convey an oblique cenfure in thefe obfervations. The tragic poet is not to let his Pe-
gafus, like the Hippogriffe of Aftolpho,
carry him to the moon ; he is to reprefent

† Theatre Grec. par Brumoy.

men

men fuch as they were ; and indeed, when
the fable and manners do not agree, great
improprieties and perfect incredibility en-
fue.

If a Grecian fable is chofen, Grecian
manners fhould accompany it. A fuperficial decorum is kept up if Agamemnon
appears a great chief ; but he fhould be a
Greek chief too, if he is to facrifice his
daughter to Diana. The fame magnanimity of fentiment might certainly have
been found in Guftavus Adolphus, and in
other generals ; but then how monftrous
would appear the great cataftrophe of the
play !

If Shakefpear had not preferved the Roman character and fentiments, in his play
of the death of Julius Cæfar, we fhould
have abhorred Brutus as an affaffin, who
by this artifice appears a tyrannicide : and
had not Mr. Addifon made Cato a patriot,
according to the Roman mode, we fhould
think he was mad for killing himfelf becaufe Cæfar was likely to become perpetual dictator.

It is difficult to fympathize with a man's
paffions, without adopting, for the time,
his

his opinions, cuftoms, and prejudices : but it is certainly neceffary to exhibit the man as ftrongly tinctured with thofe prejudices and cuftoms as poffible.

To all but fuperficial critics, would it not appear as ridiculous to fee Thefeus and Achilles wear French manners as a French drefs ? A little reflection would fhew it is more fo : for there are relations between manners and fentiments, and none between drefs and fentiment.

It is ftrange that painters, who are to give the mute inanimate figure, are required to be rigid obfervers of the Coftumi, and the dramatic poet who is to imitate fentiment, difcourfe, and action, fhould be allowed to neglect them.

O N

ON THE

HISTORICAL

D R A M A.

Nec minimum meruere decus, veftigia Græca
Auſi deſerere, et celebrare domeſtica faɛta.

ON THE

HISTORICAL

DRAMA.

THOSE dramas of Shakefpear, which
he diftinguifhes by the name of his
hiftories, being of an original kind and peculiar conftruction, cannot come within a-
ny rules which are prior to their exiftance.
The office of the critic, in regard to poetry, is like that of the grammarian and
rhetorician in refpect to the language : it
is their bufinefs to fhew why fuch and fuch
modes of fpeech are proper and graceful,
others improper and ungraceful : but they
pronounce only on fuch words and expreffions as are actually extant.

The rules of Ariftotle were drawn from
the tragedies of Æfchylus, Sophocles, &c.
Had that great critic feen a play fo fafhioned on the chronicles of his country, thus
representative

reprefentative of the manners of the times, and characters of the moft illuftrious perfons concerned in a feries of important events, perhaps he would have efteemed fuch a fort of drama well worth his attention, as very peculiarly adapted to thofe ends which the Grecian philofophers propofed in popular entertainments. If it be the chief ufe of hiftory, that it teaches philofophy by experience, this fpecies of hiftory muft be allowed to be the beft preceptor. The cataftrophe of thefe plays is not derived from a vain and idle fable of the wrath of Juno, or the revenge of flighted Bacchus; nor is a man reprefented entangled in the web of fate, from which his virtues and his deities cannot extricate him : but here we are admonifhed to obferve the confequences of pride and ambition, the tyrant's dangers and the traitor's fate. The fentiments and the manners, the paffions and their confequences, are openly expofed and immediately united: the force and luftre of poetical language join with the weight and authority of hiftory, to imprefs the moral leffon on the heart. The poet collects, as it were, into a focus thofe truths, which lie fcattered in the diffufe volume of the hiftorian,

and

and kindles the flame of virtue, while he
fhews the miferies and calamities of vice.

The common interefts of humanity make
us attentive to every ftory that has an air
of reality, but we are more affected if we
know it to be true ; and the intereft is ftill
heightened if we have any relation to the
perfons concerned. Our noble countryman, Percy, engages us much more than
Achilles, or any Grecian hero. The people for whofe ufe thefe public entertainments fhould be chiefly intended, know
the battle of Shrewfbury to be a fact : they
are informed of what has paffed on the
banks of the Severn ; all that happened
on the fhore of the Scamander has to them
the appearance of a fiction.

As the misfortunes of nations as well as
of individuals often arife from their peculiar difpofitions, cuftoms, prejudices, and
vices, thefe home born dramas are excel-
lently calculated to correct them. The
Grecian tragedies are fo much eftablifhed
on their mythology as to be very improper on our ftage. The paffion of Phædra
and the death of Hippolytus, occafioned
by the interpofition of Venus and Nep·
tune, wear the apparent marks of fiction ;

D

and

and when we ceafe to believe, we ceafe to
be affected.

The nature of the hiftorical play gave
fcope to the extenfive talents of Shakefpear. He had an uncommon felicity in
painting manners and developing characters, which he could employ with peculiar grace and propriety, when he exhibited the chiefs in our civil wars. The great
Earl of Warwick, Cardinal Beaufort, Hum-
phrey Duke of Gloucefter, the renowned
Hotfpur, were very interefting objects to
their countrymen. Whatever fhewed them
in a ftrong light, and reprefented them
with fentiments and manners agreeable to
their hiftorical characters ; and thofe things
common fame had divulged of them, muft
have engaged the attention of the fpectator, and affifted in that delufion of his
imagination from whence his fympathies
with the ftory muft arife. We are affected by the cataftrophe of a ftranger, we la-
ment the deftiny of an Œdipus, and the
misfortunes of an Hecuba ; but the little
peculiarities of character touch us only
where we have fome nearer affinity to the
perfon than the common relation of humanity : nor, unlefs we are particularly
acquainted with the original character, can
thefe

thefe diftinguifhing marks have the merit
of heightening the refemblance and ani-
mating the portrait.

We are apt to confider Shakefpear only
as a poet; but he is certainly one of the
greateft moral philofophers that ever lived.

Euripides was highly efteemed for the
moral fentences with which he has inter-
fperfed the fpeeches in his tragedies; and
certainly many general truths are expreffed
in them with a fententious brevity. But
he rather collects general opinions into
maxims, and gives them a form which is
eafily retained by memory, than extracts
any new obfervations from the characters
in action, which every reader of penetration
will find our author do continually; and
when he introduces a general maxim, it
feems forced from him by the occafion. As
it arifes out of the action, it lofes itfelf
again in it, and remains not, as in other
writers, an ambitious ornament glittering
alone, but is fo connected as to be an ufeful paffage very naturally united with the
ftory. The inftances of this are fo frequent
as to occur almoft in every fcene of his
beft plays. But left I fhould be mifun-
derftood, I will quote one from the fecond

part

part of Henry IV. where the general maxim is, that

> An habitation giddy and unfure
> Hath he that buildeth on the vulgar heart.

YORK.

                         Let us on :
And publifh the occafion of our arms
The commonwealth is fick of their own choice :
Their over greedy love hath furfeited.
An habitation giddy and unfure
Hath he that buildeth on the vulgar heart.
Oh thou fond many ! with what loud applaufe.
Did'ft thou beat heav'n with blefling Bolingbroke,
Before he was, what thou would'ft have him be !
And now, being trim'd up in thine own defires,
Thou, beaftly feeder, art fo full of him,
That thou provok'ft thyfelf to caft him up.
So, fo, thou common dog, didft thou difgorge
Thy glutton bofom of the royal Richard,
And now thou would'ft eat thy dead vomit up,
And howl'ft to find it.   What truft in thefe times?
They that when Richard liv'd would have him die,
Are now become enamour'd on his grave :
Thou that throwd'ft duft upon his goodly head,
When through proud London he came fighing on
After the admired heels of Bolingbroke,
Cry'ft now, O earth, yield us that king again,
And take thou this.

Moral reflections may be more frequent
in this kind of drama, than in the other
fpecies of tragedy, where, if not very
fhort, they teaze the fpectator, whofe mind
is intent upon, and impatient for the ca-
                                    taftrophe ;

taftrophe; and unlefs they arife neceffarily
out of the circumftances the perfon is in,
they appear unnatural. For in the preffure
of extreme diftrefs, a perfon is intent only
on himfelf, and on the prefent exigence.
The various interefts and characters in
thefe hiftorical plays, and the mixture of
the comic, weaken the operations of pity
and terror, but introduce various opportunities of conveying moral inftruction, as
occafion is given to a variety of reflections
and obfervations, more ufeful in common
life than thofe drawn from the conditions
of kings and heroes, and perfons greatly
fuperior to us by nature or fortune.

As there are poets of various talents,
and readers of various taftes, one would
rather wifh all the fields of Parnaffus might
be free and open to men of genius, than
that a proud and tyrannical fpirit of criticifm fhould controul us in the ufe of any of
them. Thofe which we fhould have judged moft barren, have brought forth noble
productions, when cultivated by an able
hand.

Even fairy land has produced the fublime; and the wild regions of romance
have

have fometimes yielded juft and genuine
fentiments.

To write a perfect tragedy, a poet muft
be poffeffed of the pathetic or the fublime ;
or perhaps to attain the utmoft excellence,
muft by a more uncommon felicity, be
able to give to the fublime the fineft
touches of paffion and tendernefs, and to
the pathetic the dignity of the fublime.
The ftraining a moderate or feeble genius
to thefe arduous tafks, has produced the
moft abfurd bombaft, and the moft pitia-
ble nonfenfe that has ever been conceived.
Ariftotle's rules, like Ulyffes' bow, are
held forth to all pretenders to tragedy,
who as unfortunate as Penelope's fuitors,
only betray their weaknefs by an attempt
fuperior to their ftrength, or ill adapted to
their faculties.   Why fhould not poetry,
in all her different forms, claim the fame
indulgence as her fifter art ? The niceft
connoiffeurs in painting have applauded
every mafter, who has juftly copied nature. Had Michael Angelo's bold pencil
been dedicated to drawing the Graces or
Rembrandt's to trace the foft bewitching
fmile of Venus, their works had probably
proved very contemptible. Fafhion does
not fo eafily impofe on our fenfes as it mifleads

leads our jubgment. Truth of defign, and
natural colouring, will always pleafe the
eye ; we appeal not here to any fet of
rules, but in an imitative art require only
juft imitation, with a certain freedom and
energy, which is always neceffary to form
a compleat refemblance to the pattern
which is borrowed from nature. I will
own, the figures of gods and goddeffes,
graceful nymphs,· and beautiful Cupids,
are finer fubjects for the pencil than ordinary human forms; yet if the painter im-
parts to thefe a refemblance to celebrated
perfons, throws them into their proper attitudes, and gives a faithful copy of the
Coftumi of the age and country, his work
will create fenfations of a different, but
not lefs pleafing kind than thofe excited
by the admiration of exquifite beauty and
perfect excellence of workmanfhip. Perhaps he fhould rather be accounted a nice
virtuofo than a confummate critic, who
prefers the poet or fculptor's faireft idea
to the various and extenfive merits of the
hiftoric reprefentation.

Nothing great is to be expected from
any fet of artifts, who are to give only co=
pies of copies. The treafures of nature
are inexhauftible, as well in moral as in
phyfical

phyfical fubjects.   The talents of Shakefpear were univerfal, his penetrating mind
faw through all characters; and, as Mr.
Pope fays of him, he was not more a mafter of our ftrongeft emotions than of our
idleft fenfations.

One cannot wonder, that endued with
fo great and various powers, he broke
down the barriers that had before confined
the dramatic writers to the regions of comedy or tragedy.   He perceived the fertility of the fubjects that lay between the
two extreams; he faw, that in the hiftorical play he could reprefent the manners
of the whole people, give the general tem·
per of the times, and bring in view the
incidents that affected the common fate of
his country.   The Gothic mufe had a rude
fpirit of liberty, and delighted in painting
popular tumults, the progrefs of civil wars,
and the revolutions of government, rather
than a cataftrophe within the walls of a
palace.   At the time he wrote, the wars
of the Houfes of York and Lancafter were
frefh in mens minds.   They had received
the tale from fome Neftor in their family,
or neighbourhood, who had fought in the
battle he related.   Every fpectator's affections were ranged under the white or red
Rofe

Rofe, in whofe contentions fome had loft
their parents and friends, others had gained eftablifhments and honours.

All the inducements which the Greek
tragedians had to chufe their heroes from
the works of the poets who had fung the
wars of Troy, and the Argonautic expe-
dition, were ftill in greater force with our
countryman to take his fubjects from the
hiftory and traditions of thofe more recent
tranfactions, in which the fpectator was informed and interefted more perfonally and
locally. There was not a family fo low,
that had not fome of its branches torn off
in the ftorms of thefe inteftine commoti-
ons : nor a valley fo happily retired, that
at fome time, *the foot of hoftile paces had
not bruis'd her flow'rets.* In thefe characters the rudeft peafant read the fad hiftory
of his country, while the better fort were
informed of the moft minute circumftances
by our chronicles. The tragedians who
took their fubjects from Homer, had all
the advantage a painter would have, who
was to draw a picture from a ftatue of
Phidias or Praxiteles. Poor Shakefpear
from the wooden images in our mean chronicles was to form his portraits. What
judgment was there in difcovering, that

by

by moulding them to an exact refemblance
he fhould engage and pleafe ! And what
difcernment and penetration into characters, and what amazing fkill in moral
painting, to be able from fuch uncouth
models, to bring forth not only a perfect,
but when occafion required, a graceful
likenefs !

The patterns from whence he drew,
were not only void of poetical fpirit and
ornament, but alfo of the hiftorical dignity.
The hiftories of thefe times were a mere
heap of rude undigefted annals, coarfe in
their ftyle, and crouded with trivial anec-
dotes. No Tacitus had inveftigated the
obliquites of our ftatefmen, or by diving
into the profound fecrets of policy had
dragged into light the latent motives, the
fecret machinations of our politicians : yet
how does he enter into the deepeft myfteries of ftate ! There cannot be a ftronger
proof of the fuperiority of his genius over
the hiftorians of the times than the following inftance.

The learned Sir Thomas More in his
hiftory of Crook'd-Back Richard, tells,
with the garrulity of an old nurfe, the
current ftories of this king's deformity,
and the monftrous appearances of his infan-
cy,

cy, which he feems with fuperftitious credulity to believe to have been the omens
and prognofticks of his future villainy.
Shakefpear with a more philofophic turn
of mind, confiders them not as prefaging,
but as inftigating his cruel ambition, and
finely accounts in the following fpeeches
for the afperity of his temper, and his
fierce and unmitigated defire of dominion,
from his being by his perfon difqualified
for the fofter engagements of fociety..

GLOUCESTER.

Well, fay there is no kingdom then for Richard :.
What other pleafure can the world afford ?
I'll make my heaven on a lady's lap ;
And deck my body in gay ornaments,
And 'witch fweet ladies with my words and looks.
Oh! miferable thought! and more unlikely,
Than to accomplifh twenty golden crowns.
Why, love forfwore me in my mother's womb,
And, for I fhould not deal in her foft laws,
She did corrupt frail nature with fome bribe
To fhrink my arm like to fome wither'd fhrub ;.
To make an envious mountain on my back,
Where fits deformity to mock my body ;
To fhape my legs of an uneven fize ;
To difproportion me in every part.
Like to a chaos, or unlick'd bear-whelp
That carries no impreffion like the dam.
And am I then a man to be belov'd ?
Oh monftrous fault to harbour fuch a thought!'
Then fince the world affords no joy to me,
But to command, to check, to o'er-bear fuch.
As are of better perfon than myfelf ;

I'll

I'll make my heav'n to dream upon the crown,
And while we live to account this world but hell,
Untill the mishap'd trunk that bears this head
Be round impaled with a glorious crown.

[Henry VI. Act 3d, Scene 3d.

GLOUCESTER.

The midwife wonder'd, and the women cry'd,
Oh Jesus bless us, he is born with teeth !
And so I was, which plainly signified
That I should snarl, and bite, and play the dog :
Then since the heavens have shap'd my body so,
Let hell make crook'd my mind to answer it.
I have no brother, I am like no brother,
And that word, love, which grey-beards call divine,
Be resident in men like one another,
And not in me : I am myself alone.

[Henry VI. Act 5th, Scene 7th.

Our author by following minutely the
chronicles of the times has embarrassed his
dramas with too great a number of persons
and events. The hurley-burley of these
plays recommended them to a rude illiterate audience, who, as he says, loved a
noise of targets. His poverty, and the low
condition of the stage (which at that time
was not frequented by persons of rank)
obliged him to this complaisance ; and un-
fortunately he had not been tutored by
any rules of art, or informed by acquaintance with just and regular dramas. Even
the politer sort by reading books of chivalry,

ry, which were the polite literature of the
times, were accuſtomed to bold adventures and atchievments. In our northern
climates heroic adventures pleaſed more
than the gallant dialogue, where love and
honour diſpute with all the ſophiſtry of the
ſchools, and one knows not when the con-
teſt would end, if heraldry did not ſtep
in and decide the point, as in the ſoliloquy of the Infanta in the Cid.

> L'INFANTE.
> T'écoutrai-je encor, reſpeĉt de ma naiſſance,,
>   Qui fais un crime de mes feux ?
> T'écouterai-je, amour, dont la douce puiſſance
> Contre ce fier tyran fait rebeller mes vœux ?
>   Pauvre princeſſe, auquel des deux
>   Dois-tu prêter obéiſſance ?
> Rodrigue, ta valeur te rend digne de moi ;
> Mais pour être vaillant tu n'es pas fils de roi.
>   Le Cid, Aĉte 5me.

Nor is this rule, that a princeſs can love
only the ſon of a king, a mere Spaniſh
punto; you ſhall hear two Spartan virgins,
daughters of Lyſander, ſpeaking the ſame
language.

> ELPINICE.
> Cotys eſt roi, ma ſœur ; & comme ſa couronne
>   Parle ſuffiſamment pour lui,
> Aſſuré de mon cœur que ſon trône lui donne,
> De le trop demander il s'épargne l'ennui.

This

This lady then proceeds to queſtion her ſiſter concerning her inclination for her lover Spitridates, and urges in his favour;

ELPINICE.

Car enfin, Spitridate a l'entretien charmant,
L'œil vif, l'eſprit aiſé, le cœur bon, l'ame belle ;
A tant de qualités s il joignoit un vrai zéle.

To which the other anſwers,

AGLATIDE.

Ma ſœur, il n'eſt pas roi comme l'eſt votre amant.
Il n'eſt pas roi, vous dis-je, & c'eſt un grand defaut *.

The Queen of the Luſitanians, in the famous play of Sertorius, ſpeaks thus to that Roman general ;

VIRITATE

Car enfin pour remplir l'honneur de ma naiſſance,
Il me faudroit un roi de titre, & de puiſſance ;
Mais comme il n'en eſt plus, je penſe m'en devoir,
Ou le pouvoir ſans nom, ou le nom ſans pouvoir.

And upon the effect of this prudent deciſion turns the great intereſt of the play. By the laws of Romance the men are to be amorous, and the ladies ambitious. Poor Sertorius in his old age is in love with this lady, for whom Perpenna is alſo dying ; and Sertorius whom we had ſuppoſed ſacrificed to the ambition of his lieutenant, is the victim of his jealouſy.

Shakeſpear

* Ageſilaus of Corneille.

Shakefpear and Corneille are equally blameable, for having complied with the bad tafte of the age; and by doing fo, they have both brought unmerited cenfures on their country. The French impute barbarity and cruelty, to a people that could delight in bloody fkirmifhes on the ftage. The Englifh, as unjuftly, but as excufa bly, accufe of effeminacy and frivoloufnefs, thofe who could fit to hear the following addrefs of a lover to his miftrefs's bodkin, with which fhe had juft put out one of his eyes:

PYMANTE.

O toi, qui fecondant fon courage inhumain,
Loin d'orner fes cheveux, defhonores fa main,
Exécrable inftrument de fa brutale rage,
Tu devais pour le moins refpeéter fon image :
Ce portrait accompli d'un chef-d'œuvre des cieux ;
Imprimé dans mon cœur, exprimé dans mes yeux,
Quoi que te comnandât une ame fi cruelle,
Devait être adoré de ta pointe rebelle.

Clitandre de Corneille.

The whole foliloquy includes feventy lines. I heartily wifh for the honour of both nations, the lover and his bodkin, and the foldiers and their halberds, had always been hiffed off the ftage. Our countryman was betrayed into his error by want of judgment, to difcern what part of

his

his ſtory was not fit for repreſentation.
Corneille, for want of dramatic genius,
was obliged to have recourſe to points,
conceits, cold and uninterefting declamations to fill up his plays, and theſe heavily
drag along his undramatical dramas to a
fifth act.

The ignorance of the times paſſed over
the defects of each author; and the bad
taſte then prevalent did more than endure,
it even encouraged and approved what
ſhould have been cenſured.

Mr. Voltaire has ſaid, that the plots of
Shakeſpear's plays are as wild as that of
the Clitandre juſt quoted; and it muſt be
allowed they are often exceptionable, but
at the ſame time we muſt obſerve, that
though crowded too much, they are not ſo
perplexed as to be unintelligible, which
Corneile confeſſes his Clitandre might be
to thoſe who ſaw it but once. There is
ſtill another more eſſential difference perhaps, which is, that the wildeſt and moſt
incorrect pieces of our poet contain ſome
incomparable ſpeeches: whereas the worſt
plays of Corneille have not a good ſtanza.
The tragedy of King Lear is very far from
being a regular piece, yet there are ſpeeches
in

in it which perhaps excel any thing that
has been written by any tragedian, ancient
or modern.   However we will only compare one paſſage of it at preſent, with a-
nother in Clitandre ; as they both happen
to be on ſimilar ſubjeċts.   The blinded
lover,   after many complaints, and wiſhes
for revenge, hears the noiſe of a tempeſt,
and thus he breaks out :

Pymante.

Mes menaces déja ſont trembler tout le monde :
Le vent fuit d'épouvante, et le tonnetre en gronde :
L'œil du ciel s'en retire, et par un voile noir,
N'y pouvant réſiſter, ſe défend d'en rien voir.
Cent nuages épais ſe diſtilant en larmes,
A force de pitié, veulant m'oter les armes.
La nature etonnée embraſſe mon couroux,
Et veut m'offrir Doriſe, ou devancer mes coups.
Tout eſt de mon parti, le ciel même n'envoie
Tant d'éclairs redoublés, qu'afin que je la voie.

King Lear, whom age renders weak
and querulous, and who is now beginning
to grow mad, thus very naturally, in the
general calamity of the ſtorm, recurs to
his own particular circumſtances.

Lear.

Spit fire, ſpout rain ;
Nor rain, wind, thunder, fire, are my daughters ;
I tax you not, ye elements, with unkindneſs,
I never gave you kingdoms, call'd you children,

You

You owe me no fubmiffion.   Then let fall
Your horrible pleafure ; here I ftand your flave,
A poor, infirm, weak, and defpis'd old man !
And yet I call you fervile minifters,
That have with two pernicious daughters join'd
Your high engender'd battles, 'gainft a head
So old and white as this.   Oh! oh ! 'tis foul.

They muft have little feeling that are not
touched by this fpeech fo highly pathetic.

How fine is that which follows!

LEAR.
            Let the great Gods,
That keep this dreadful pother o'er our heads,
Find out their enemies now. Tremble thou wretch,
That haft within thee undivulged crimes
Unwhipt of juftice ! Hide thee thou bloody hand,
Thou perjur'd, and thou fimular of virtue,
That art inceftuous !   Caitiff, fhake to pieces,
That under covert, and convenient feeming,
Haft practis'd on man's life ! Clofe pent up guilts,
Rive your concealing continents, and afk
Thefe dreadful fummoners grace !—I am a man
More finn'd againft than finning.

Thus it is Shakefpear redeems the nonfenfe, the indecorums, the irregularities
of his plays ; and whoever, for want of
natural tafte, or ignorance in the Englifh
language, is infenfible to the merit of thefe
paffages, is juft as unfit to judge of his
works, as a deaf man, who only perceived

ed the blacknefs of the fky, and did not
hear the deep-voiced thunder, and the
roaring elements, would have been to have
defcribed the awful horrors of this midnight ftorm.

The French critic apologizes for our
perfifting in the reprefentation of Shakefpear's plays, by faying we have none of
a more regular form. In this he is extreme-
ly miftaken; we have many plays written
according to the rules of art; but nature,
which fpeaks in Shakefpear, prevails over
them all. If at one of our theatres there
was a fet of actors who gave the true force
of every fentiment, expreffed juftly every
emotion of the heart, feemed infpired with
the paffion they were to counterfeit, fell
fo naturally into the circumftances and
fituations the poet had appointed for them,
that they never betrayed they were actors,
but fometimes would have an aukward gefture, or for a moment a vicious pronunciation, fhould we not conftantly refort thither ?—If at another theatre there were a
fet of puppets regularly featured, exactly
proportioned, whofe movements were geo-
metricaly juft, that fpoke through an or-
gan fo conftituted by a great mafter of
mufic as never to give any harfh or difa-
greeable

greeable tones, and the faces, the action, pronunciation of thefe puppets had no fault, but that there was no expreffion in their countenance, no natural air in their motion, and that their fpeech had not the various inflexions of the human voice, would a real connoiffeur abandon the living actors for fuch lifelefs images, becaufe fome nice and dainty critic pleaded, that the puppets were not fubject to any human infirmities, would not cough, fneeze, or become hoarfe in the midft of a fine period? or could it avail much to urge their movements and tones, being directed by juft mechanics, would never betray the aukwardnefs of rufticity, or a falfe accent caught from bad education.

Shakefpear's dramatis perfonæ are men, frail by conftitution, hurt by ill habits, faulty and unequal. But they fpeak with human voices, are actuated by human paffions, and are engaged in the common affairs of human life. We are interefted in what they do, or fay, by feeling every moment, that they are of the fame nature as ourfelves. Their precepts therefore are an inftruction, their fates and fortunes an experience, their teftimony an authority, and their misfortunes a warning.

Love

Love and ambition are the fubjects of the French plays. From the firft of thefe paffions many from age and temper are entirely exempted ; and from the fecond many more, by fituation are excluded. Among a thoufand fpectators, there are not perhaps half a dozen, who ever were, or can be, in the circumftances of the perfons reprefented : they cannot fympathize with them, unlefs they have fome conception of a tender paffion, combated by ambition, or ambition ftruggling with love. The fable of the French plays is often taken from hiftory, but then a romantic paffion is added to it, and to which both events and characters are rendered fubfervient.

Shakefpear, in various nature wife, does not confine himfelf to any particular paffion. When he writes from hiftory, he attributes to the perfons fuch fentiments as agreed with their actions and characters. There is not a more fure way of judging of the merit of rival geniufes, than to bring them to the teft of comparifon where they have attempted fubjects that have any refemblance. Corneille appears much inferior to our Shakefpear in the, art of conducting the events, and difplaying the

characters

characters he borrows from the historian's page; his tragedy of Otho comprehends that period in which his courtiers are caballing to make him adopt a succeffor agreeable to their interefts.

The court of that emperor is finely defcribed by Tacitus, who in a few words fets before us the infolence, the profligacy, and rapacioufnefs of a fet of minifters, encouraged by the weaknefs of the prince to attempt whatever they wifhed, and incited by his age to fnatch by hafty rapine whatever they coveted.——Tacitus, with his mafterly pencil, has drawn the outlines of their characters fo ftrongly that a writer of any genius might finifh up the portraits to great refemblance and perfection.   One had furely a right to expect this from an author, who profeffes to have copied this great hiftorian the moft faithfully that was poffible.   One would imagine the infolent Martianus, the bold and fubtle Vinius, the bafe, fcandalous, flothful Laco fhould all appear in their proper characters, which would be unfolding through the whole progrefs of the play,   as their various fchemes and interefts were expofed. Inftead of this Martianus makes fubmiffive love: Vinius and Laco are two ambitious courtiers,

tiers, without any quality that diftinguifhes them from each other, or from any other intriguing ftatefman; nor do they at all contribute to bring about the revolution in the empire : their whole bufinefs feems to be matchmaking, and in that too they are fo unfkilful as not to fucceed. They undertake it indeed, merely as it may influence the adoption. Several fentences from Tacitus are ingrafted into the dialogues, but, from a change of perfons and circumftances, they lofe much of their original force and beauty.

Galba addreffes to his niece, who is in love with Otho, the fine fpeech which the hiftorian fuppofes him to have made to Pifo when he adopted him. The lovefick lady, tired of an harangue, the purport of which is unfavourable to her lover, and being befides no politician, anfwers the emperor, that fhe does not underftand ftate-affairs : a cruel reply to a fpeech he could have no motive for making, but to difplay his wifdom and eloquence. The old warrior is more complaifant to her, for he enters into all the delicacies of her paffion, as if he had ftudied la carte du tendre*. To fteal fo much matter from Tacitus

---

* Roman de Clelie.

citus without imbibing one fpark of his fpirit; to tranflate whole fpeeches, yet preferve no likenefs in the characters, is furely betraying a great deficiency of dramatic powers, and of the art of imitation : to reprefent the gay, luxurious, diffolute, ambitious Otho, the courtier of Nèro, and the gallant of Poppea, as a mere Paftor Fido, who would die rather than be inconftant to his miftrefs, and is indifferent to empire but for her fake, is fuch a violation of hiftorical truth, as is not to be endured. I pafs over the abfurd fcene between the jealous ladies, the improbability of their treating the powerful and haughty favourites of the emperor with indignity, and Otho's thrice repeated attempt to kill himfelf before his miftrefs's face without the leaft reafon why he fhould put an end to his life, or probability that fhe would fuffer him to do it. To make minute criticifms where the great parts are fo defective would be trifling.

Having obferved how poorly Corneille has reprefented characters borrowed from fo great a portrait painter as Tacitus, let us now fee what Shakefpear has done, from thofe aukward originals, our old chronicles.

O N

ON THE

FIRST PART

OF

HENRY IV.

E

THE

FIRST PART

O F

HENRY IV.

THE peculiar dexterity with which the author unfolds the characters, and prepares the events of this play, deferves our attention.

There is not, perhaps, any thing more difficult in the whole compafs of the dramatic art, than to open to the fpectator the previous incidents that were productive of the prefent circumftances, and the characters of the perfons from whofe conduct in fuch circumftances, the fubfequent events are to flow. An intelligent fpectator will receive great pleafure from obferving every action naturally arifing out of

E 2   the

the fentiments and manners of the perfons
reprefented. Happier is the poet, the
perplexities of whofe fable are unfolded by
the natural operation of the difpofitions of
the perfons who compofe it, than even he,
to whom it is permitted to call a deity to
his affiftance. This play opens by the
king's declaring his intention to undertake
the crufade, as foon as peace will allow
him to do it. Weftmorland informs him
of the defeat of Mortimer by Owen Glendower; the king relates the news of Percy's
victory at Holmedon, which naturally
leads him to the praife of this young hero,
and to exprefs an envy of Lord Northumberland's happinefs.

> To be the father of fo bleft a fon,
> While I (fays he)
> See riot and difhonour ftain the brow
> Of my young Harry :

then he mentions Percy's refufal of his pri-
foners, which Weftmorland attributes to
the malevolent fuggeftions of Worcefter.
Thus at once is prefented to the fpectator,
the condition of the ftate, the temper of
the times, and the characters of the perfons from whence the cataftrophe is to
arife.

The ftern authority the king affumes on
Hotfpur's difobedience to his commands,
could

coůld not fail to inflame a warm young
hero fluſhed with recent victory, and elate
with the conſciouſneſs of having ſo well
defended a crown, which his father and
uncle had in a manner conferred. Nothing can be more natural than that, in
ſuch a temper, he ſhould recur to the obligations the king had received from his
family : and thus while he ſeems venting
his ſpleen, he explains to the ſpectator
what is paſt, and opens the ſource of the
future rebellion ; and by connecting former tranſactions with the preſent paſſions
and events, creates in the reader an intereſt and a ſympathy, which a cold narration or a pompous declamation could
not have effected. As the Author deſigned Percy ſhould be an intereſting character,
his diſobedience to the king, in regard to
the priſoners, is mitigated by his pleading the unfitneſs of the perſon and unfa-
vorableneſs of the occaſion to urge him
on the ſubject. To this effeminate courtier (ſays he)

> I then, all ſmarting with my wounds being cold,
> Out of my grief and my impatience
> To be ſo peſter'd with a popinjay,
> Anſwered neglectingly—I know not what.

Thus has the poet diveſted the rebel of
the hateful crimes of premeditated revolt

E 3   and

and deep-laid treachery. He is hurried
by an impetuoſity of ſoul out of the ſphere
of obedience, and, like a comet, though
dangerous to the general ſyſtem, he is
ſtill an object of admiration and wonder
to every beholder. It is marvellous, that
Shakeſpear from bare chronicles, coarſe
hiſtory, and traditional tales, could thus
extract the wiſdom and caution of the politician Henry, and catch the fire of the
martial ſpirit of Hotſpur. The wrath of
Achilles in Homer is not ſuſtained with
more dignity. Each hero is offended that
the prize of valour,

> Due to many a well-fought day.

is rudely ſnatched from him by the hand
of power. One ſhould ſuſpect an author
of more learning to have had the character
of Achilles in his eye, and alſo the advice
of Horace in the manner of repreſenting
him on the ſtage.

> Impiger, iracundus, inexorabilis, acer.
> Jura neget ſibi nata, nihil non arroget armis.

His miſdemeanors riſe ſo naturally out
of his temper, and that temper is ſo noble,
that we are almoſt as much intereſted for
him as for a more virtuous character.

His

His treſpaſs may be well forgot,
It hath th' excuſe of youth and heat of blood,
And an adopted name of privilege,
A hare-brain'd Hotſpur govern'd by a ſpleen.

The great aſpiring ſoul of Hotſpur bears
out rebellion : it ſeems, in him, to flow
from an uncontrollable energy of ſoul,
born to give laws, too potent to receive
them. In every ſcene he appears with
the ſame animation ; he is always that
Percy

Whoſe ſpirit lent a fire
Even to the dulleſt peaſant in the camp,
Led ancient lords and rev'rend biſhops on
To bloody battles, and to bruiſing arms.

He has too the frankneſs of Achilles,
and the ſame abhorrence of falſhood ; he
is as impatient of Glendower's pretenſions
to ſupernatural powers, as to the king's
aſſuming a right over his priſoners. In
dividing the kingdom he will not yield a
foot of ground to thoſe who diſpute with
him ; but would give any thing to a well-
deſerving friend. It is a pardonable violation of hiſtorical truth, to give the Prince
of Wales, who behaved very gallantly at
the battle of Shrewſbury, the honour of
conquering him ; and it is more agreeable
to the ſpectator, as the event was, to beat
down

The never-daunted Percy to the earth.

E 4　　　　　　　　　　to

to suppose it did not happen from the arrow of a peasant, but from the sword of Henry Monmouth, whose spirit came with a higher commission from the same fiery sphere.

In Worcester the rebel appears in all his odious colours ; proud, envious, malignant, artful, he is finely contrasted by the noble Percy. Shakespear, with the sagacity of a Tacitus, observes the jealousies which must arise between a family, which has conferred a crown, and the king who has received it, who will always think the presence of such benefactors *too bold and peremptory.*

The character of Henry IV. is perfectly agreeable to that given him by historians. The play opens by his declaring his intentions to war against the infidels, which he does not undertake, as was usual in those times, from a religious enthusiasm, but is induced to it by political motives : that the martial spirit may not break out at home in civil wars ; nor peace and idleness give men opportunity to enquire into his title to the crown, and too much discuss a point which would not bear a cool and close examination. Henry had the
                                   specious

ſpecious talents, which aſſiſt a man under
certain circumſtances to uſurp a kingdom,
but either from the want of thoſe great
and ſolid qualities, which are neceſſary to
maintain opinion loyal to the throne to
which it had raiſed him, or from the im-
poſſibility of ſatisfying the expectations of
thoſe who had aſſiſted his uſurpation, as
ſome of the beſt hiſtorians with great appearance of reaſon have ſuggeſted *, it is
certain his reign was full of diſcontents and
troubles.

The popular arts by which he captivated the multitude, are finely deſcribed in
the ſpeech he makes to his ſon, in the third
act.   Any other poet would have thought
he had acquitted himſelf well enough in
that dialogue, by a general fatherly admonition delivered with the dignity be-
comming a monarch: but Shakeſpear rarely deals in common-place and general
morals.   The peculiar temper and circumſtances of the perſon, and the exigency of the time, influence the ſpeaker
as in real life.   It is not only the king and
parent, but Henry Plantagenet, that chides
the prince of Wales.   How natural is it

* Hume's Hiſt. of H. IV.

E 5   for

for him, on Percy's revolt, to recur to his
own rebellion againſt Richard, and to ap-
prehend that the ſame levities which loſt
that king, firſt the opinion, then the allegiance of his ſubjeᴄts, ſhould deprive the
prince of his ſucceſſion! Nothing can be
better imagined than the parallel he draws
between himſelf and Percy, Richard and
Henry of Monmouth. The affeᴄtionate
father, the offended king, the provident
politician, and the conſcious uſurper, are
all united in the following ſpeeches:

K. HENRY.

I know not, whether God will have it ſo,
For ſome diſpleaſing ſervice I have done,
That, in his ſecret doom, out of my blood
He'll breed revengement, and a ſcourge for me.
But thou do'ſt in thy paſſages of life,
Make me believe that thou art only mark'd
For the hot vengeance and the rod of heav'n,
To puniſh my miſ-treadings. Tell me, elſe
Could ſuch inordinate and low deſires,
Such poor, ſuch baſe, ſuch lewd, ſuch mean at-
    tempts,
Such barren pleaſures, rude ſociety
As thou art match'd withal, and grafted to,
Acompany the greatneſs of thy blood,
And hold their level with thy princely heart?

K. HENRY.

Heav'n pardon thee. Yet let me wonder, Harry,
At thy affeᴄtions, which do hold a wing
Quite from the flight of all thy anceſtors.
Thy place in council thou haſt rudely loſt.
Which

Which by thy younger brother is fupply'd ;
And art almoft an alien to the hearts
Of all the court and princes of my blood.
The hope and expectation of thy time
Is ruin'd, and the foul of every man
Prophetically does fore-think thy fall.
Had I fo lavifh of my prefence been,
So common-hackney'd in the eyes of men,,
So fteal and cheap to vulgar company ;
Opinion, that did help me to the crown,
Had ftill kept loyal to poffeffion,
And left me in reputelefs banifhment,
A fellow of no mark, nor likelihood.
But being feldom feen, I could not ftir,
But, like a comet, I was wonder'd at,
That men would tell their children, this is he ;
Others would fay, where ? which is Bolingbroke ?
And then I ftole all courtefy from heav'n,
And dreft myfelf in much humility,
That I did pluck allegiance from mens hearts,
Loud fhouts and falutations from their mouths,
Even in the prefence of the crowned king.
Thus I did keep my perfon frefh and new,
My prefence, like a robe pontifical,
Ne'er feen, but wonder'd at ; and fo my ftate,
Seldom, but fumptuous, fhew'd like a feaft,
And won, by rarenefs, fuch folemnity.
The fkipping king, he ambled up and down
With fhallow jefters, and rafh bavin wits,
Soon kindled, and foon burnt ; 'fcarded his ftate,
Mingled his royalty with carping fools ;
Had his great name profaned with their fcorns ;
And gave his countenance, againft his name,
To laugh at gybing boys, and ftand the pufh
Of every beardlefs, vain comparative ;
Grew a companion to the common ftreets,
Enfeoff'd himfelf to popularity.
That, being daily fwallowed by mens eyes,

They

They furfeited with honey, and began
To loath a tafte of fweetnefs ; whereof a little
More than a little, is by much too much.
So when he had occafion to be feen ;
He was but as cuckow is in June,
Heard, not regarded; feen, but with fuch eyes,
As, fick and blunted with community,
Afford no extraordinary gaze ;
Such, as is bent on fun-like majefty,
When it fhines feldom in admiring eyes ;
But rather drowz'd, and hung their eye-lids down,
Slept in his face, and render'd fuch afpect
As cloudy men ufe to their adverfaries,
Being with his prefence glutted, gorg'd and full.
And in that very line, Harry, ftand'ft thou ;
For thou haft loft thy princely privilege
With vile participation; not an eye,
But is a-weary of thy common fight,
Save mine, which hath defired to fee thee more ;
Which now doth, what I would not have it do,
Make blind itfelf with foolifh tendernefs.

Our author is fo little under the difcipline of art, that we are apt to afcribe
his happieft fuccefles, as well as his moft
unfortunate failings, to chance. But I
cannot help thinking, there is more of
contrivance and care in his execution of
this play, than in almoft any he has written. It is a more regular drama than his
other hiftorical plays, lefs charged with
abfurdities, and lefs involved in confufion.
It is indeed liable to thofe objections which
are made to tragi-comedy. But if the pedantry

dantry of learning could ever recede from
its dogmatical rules, I think that this play
inftead of being condemned for being of
that fpecies, would obtain favour for the
fpecies itfelf, though perhaps correct tafte
may be offended with the tranfitions from
grave and important, to light and ludicrous fubjects, and more ftill with thofe
from great and illuftrious, to low and mean
perfons. Foreigners unufed to thefe compofitions, will be much difgufted at them.
The vulgar call all animals that are not
natives of their own country, monfters,
however beautiful they may be in their
form, or wifely adapted to their climate
and natural deftination. The prejudices
of pride are as violent and unreafonable as
the fuperftitions of ignorance. On the
French Parnaffus, a tragi-comedy of this
kind will be deemed a monfter fitter to be
fhewn to the people at a fair, than exhibited to circles of the learned and polite.
From fome peculiar circumftances relating
to the characters in the piece, we may,
perhaps, find a fort of apology for the
motley mixture thrown into it. We cannot but fuppofe, that at the time it was
written, many ftories yet fubfifted of the
wild adventures of this Prince of Wales,
and his idle companions. His fubfequent
refor-

reformation, and his conqueſts in France,
rendered him a very popular character.
It was a delicate affair to expoſe the follies
of Henry V. before a people proud of his
victories, and tender of his fame, at the
ſame time ſo informed of the extravagancies and exceſſes of his youth, that he
could not appear diveſted of them with
any degree of hiſtorical probability Their
enormity would have been greatly heightened, if they had appeared in a piece entirely ſerious and full of dignity and decorum.
How happily therefore was the character
of Falſtaffe introduced, whoſe wit and
feſtivity in ſome meaſure excuſe the Prince
for admitting him into his familiarity, and
ſuffering himſelf to be led by him into
ſome irregularities.   There is hardly a
young hero, full of gaiety and ſpirits,
who, if he had once fallen into the ſociety
of ſo pleaſant a companion, could have the
ſeverity to diſcard him, or would not ſay,
as the Prince does,

He could better ſpare a better man.

How ſkilfully does our author follow the
tradition of the Prince's having been engaged in a robbery, yet make his part in
it a mere frolic, to play on the cowardly
and braggart temper of Falſtaffe ! The
whole

whole conduct of that incident is very artful : he rejects the propoſals of the robbery,
and only complies with playing a trick on
the robbers ; and care is taken to inform
you, that the money is returned to its
owners.——The Prince ſeems always diverted, rather than ſeduced by Falſtaffe ;
he deſpiſes his vices while he is entertain-
ed by his humour : and though Falſtaffe
is for a while a ſtain upon his character,
yet it is of a kind with thoſe colours which
are uſed for a diſguiſe in ſport, being of
ſuch a nature as are eaſily waſhed out,
without leaving any bad tincture. And
we ſee Henry, as ſoon as he is called to
the high and ſerious duties of a king, come
forth at once with an unblemiſhed majeſty.
The diſpoſition of the hero is made to
pierce through the idle frolicks of the boy,
throughout the whole play ; for his reformation is not effected in the laſt ſcene of
the laſt act, as is uſual in our comedies,
but is prepared from the very beginning
of the play. The ſcene between the Prince
and Francis, is low and ridiculous, and
ſeems one of the greateſt indecorums in
the piece ; at the ſame time the attentive
ſpectator will find the purpoſe of it is to
ſhew him, that Henry was ſtudying human nature in all her variety of tempers
                                    and

and faculties. I am now, fays he, acquainted with all humours (meaning difpofitions) fince the days of good man
Adam to the prefent hour. In the play
of Henry V. you are told, that in his youth
he had been feduloufly obferving mankind ; and from an apprehenfion, perhaps,
how difficult it was to acquire an intimate
knowlege of men, whilft he kept up the
forms his rank prefcribed, he waved the
ceremonies and decorums of his fituation,
and familiarly converfed with all orders of
fociety.——The jealoufy his father had
conceived of him would probably have
been increafed, if he had affected fuch a
fort of popularity as would have gained
the efteem and love of the multitude.

Whether Henry in the early part of his
life was indulging a humour that inclined
him to low and wild company, as endea-
vouring to acquire a deeper and more extenfive knowledge of human nature, by a
general acquaintance with mankind, it is
the bufinefs of his hiftorians to determine.
But a critic muft furely applaud the dexterity of Shakefpear for throwing this colour over that part of his conduct, whether
he feized on fome intimations hiftorians
had given of that fort, or, of himfelf imagined

gined ſo reſpectable a motive for the
Prince's deviations from the dignity of his
birth.   This piece muſt have delighted
the people at the time it was written, as
the follies of their favourite character were
ſo managed, that they rather ſeemed foils
to ſet off its virtues, than ſtains which
obſcured them.

Whether we conſider the character of
Falſtaffe as adapted to encourage and excuſe the extravagancies of the Prince, or
by itſelf, we muſt certainly admire it, and
own it to be perfectly original.

The profeſſed wit, either in life or on
the ſtage, is uſually ſevere and ſatirical.
But mirth is the ſource of Falſtaffe's wit.
He ſeems rather to invite you to partake
of his meriment, than to attend to his
jeſt; a perſon muſt be ill natured, as well
as dull who does not join in the mirth of
this jovial companion, who is in all reſpects
the beſt calculated to raiſe laughter of any
that ever appeared on a ſtage.

He joins the fineſſe of wit with the
drollery of humour. Humour is a kind of
groteſque wit, ſhaped and coloured by the
diſpoſitions of the people in whom it re-
ſides,

ſides, or by the ſubject to which it is applied. It is ofteneſt found in odd and irregular minds : but this peculiar turn diſtorts wit, and though it gives it a burleſque air, which excites momentary, mirth, renders it leſs juſt, and conſequently leſs agreeable to our judgments. Gluttony, corpulency and cowardice, are the peculiarities of Falſtaffe's compoſition, they render him ridiculous without folly, throw an air of jeſt and feſtivity about him, and make his manners ſuit with his ſentiments, without giving to his underſtanding any particular bias. As the contempt attendant on theſe vices and defects, is the beſt antidote againſt any infection that might be caught in his ſociety, ſo it was very ſkilful to make him as ridiculous as witty, and as contemptible as entertaining. The admirable ſpeech upon honour would have been both indecent and dangerous from any other perſon. We muſt every where allow his wit is juſt, his humour genuine, and his character perfectly original, and ſuſtained through every ſcene, in every play, in which it appears.

As Falſtaffe, whom the author certainly intended to be perfectly witty, is leſs addicted to quibble and play on words,

than

than any of his comic characters, I think
we may fairly conclude, our author was
sensible it was but a false kind of wit,
which he practised from the hard necessity
of the times : for in that age, the pro-
fessor quibbled in his chair, the judge quibbled on the bench, the prelate quibbled
in the pulpit, the statesman quibbled at
the council-board ; · nay, even majesty
quibbled on the throne.

T H E

THE

SECOND PART

OF

HENRY IV.

THE

SECOND PART

OF

HENRY IV.

IT is uncommon to find the fame fpirit and intereft diffufed through the fequel as in the firft part of a play: but the fertile and happy mind of Shakefpear could create or diverfify at pleafure; could produce new characters or vary the attitudes of thofe before exhibited according to the occafion. He leaves us in doubt, whether moft to admire the fecundity of his imagination in the variety of its productions, or the ftrength and fteadinefs of his genius in fuftaining the fpirit, and preferving unim aired, through various circumftances and fituations, what his invention had originally produced.

We

We fhall hardly find any man to-day,
more like to what he was yefterday, than
the perfons here are like to what they were
in the firft part of Henry IV. This is
the more aftonifhing, as the author has
not confined himfelf, as all other dramatic
writers have done, to a certain theatrical
chara&ter ; which, formed entirely of one
paffion, prefents to us always the patriot,
the lover, or the conqueror. Thefe, ftill
turning on the fame hinge, defcribe, like
a piece of clock-work, a regular circle of
movements. In human nature, of which
Shakefpear's chara&ters are a juft imitation, every paffion is controlled and forced
into many deviations by various incidental
difpofitions and humours. The operations of this complicated machine are far
more difficult to trace, than the fteady un-
deviating line of the artificial chara&ter,
formed on one fimple principle. Our
poet feems to have as great an advantage
over ordinary dramatic poets, as Dædalus
had above his predeceffors in fculpture.
They could make a reprefentation of the
limbs and features which compofe the human form, he firft had the fkill to give it
gefture, attitude, the eafy graces of real
life, and exhibit its powers in a variety of
exertions.

We

We fhall again fee Northumberland timid and wavering, forward in confpiracy,
yet hefitating to join in an action of doubtful iffue.

King Henry is as prudent a politician
on his death-bed as at council; his eye,
juft before it clofed for ever, ftretching itfelf beyond the hour of death, to the view
of thofe dangers, which from the temper
of the Prince of Wales, and the condition
of the times, threatened his throne and
family. I cannot help taking notice of the
remarkable attention of the poet to the
cautious and politic temper of Henry,
when he makes him, even in fpeaking to
his friends and partifans, diffemble fo far,
in relating Richard's prophecy, that Northumberland who helped him to the
throne, would one day revolt from him,
as to add,

Though then, heaven knows, I had nofuch intent;
But that neceffity fo bow'd the ftate.
That I and greatnefs were compell'd to kifs.

To his fucceffor he expreffes himfelf
very differently when he fays,

Heaven knows, my fon,
By what by-paths and indirect crook'd ways
I met this crown.

F   Thefe

Thefe delicacies of conduct lie hardly within the poet's province, but have their fource in that great and univerfal capacity, which the attentive reader will find to belong to our author beyond any other writer. He alone, perhaps, would have perceived the decorum and fitnefs of making fo wife a man referved even with his friends, and truft a confeffion of the iniquities by which he obtained the crown, only to his fucceffor, whofe intereft it was not to difgrace whatever could authorize his attainment of it. Let tragedy-writers, who make princes prate with pages and waiting-women, of their murders and treafons, learn for once, from rude and illiterate Shakefpear, how averfe pride is, coolly to confefs, and prudence to betray, what the fever and deliriums of ambition had prompted to do.

Falftaffe appears with his former difpofitions, but in new fituations ; and entertains us in a variety of fcenes.

Hotfpur is as it were revived to the fpectator in the following character given of him by his lady, when fhe diffuades Northumberland from joining the forces of the archbifhop.

Lady

Lady PERCY.

Oh, yet for heav'n's fake, go not to thefe wars.
The time was, father, that you broke your word,
When you were more endear'd to it than now ;
When your own Percy, when my heart-dear Harry,
Threw many a northward look, to fee his father,
Bring up his pow'rs ; but he did long in vain !
Who then perfuaded you to ftay at home ?
There were two honours loft ; yours and your fon's.
For yours, may heavenly glcry brighten it !
For his, it ftruck upon him as the fun
In the grey vault of heav'n; and by his light
Did all the chivalry of England move
To do brave acts.　He was indeed the glafs
Wherein the noble youth did drefs themfelves.
He had no legs, that practifed not his gait ;
And fpeaking thick, which nature made his blemifh,
Became the accents of the valiant ;
For thofe that could fpeak low and tardily,
Would turn their own perfection to abufe,
To feem like him: So that in fpeech, in gait,
In diet, in affections of delight,
In military rules, humours of blood,
He was the mark and glafs, copy and book,
That fafhion'd others.　And him, wond'rous him!
O miracle of men ! him did you leave
To look upon the hideous god of war
In difadvantage ; to abide a field
Where nothing but the found of Hotfpur's name
Did feem defenfible.　So you left him.
Never, O, never do his ghoft the wrong.
To hold your honour more precife and nice
With others, than with him.　Let them alone :
The marfhal and the archbifhop are ftrong.
Had my fweet Harry had but half their numbers,
To day might I (hanging on Hotfpur's neck)
Have talk'd of Monmouth's grave.

F 2　　　　　　Juftice

Juftice Shallow is an admirably well drawn comic character, but he never appears better, than by reflection in the mirror of Falflaffe's wit, in whofe defcriptions he is moft ftrongly exhibited.—It is faid by fome, that the Juftice was meant for a particular gentleman who had profecuted the author for deer-ftealing, I know not whether that ftory be well grounded. The Shallows are to be found every where, in every age, but thofe who have leaft character of their own, are moft formed and modified by the fafhion of the times, and their peculiar profeffion or calling. So though we often meet with a refemblance to this Juftice, we fhall never find an exact parrallel to him, now manners are fo much changed.—The fuperior danger of a rebellion fanctified by the church, cannot by hiftorians or philofophers be better fet forth, than by the following words of Morton:

MORTON.

The gentle Archbifhop of York is up
With well appointed powers.   He is a man,
Who with a double furety binds his followers.
My lord, your fon had only but the corps,
But fhadows, and the fhews of men to fight;
For that fame word, rebellion did divide
The action of their bodies from their fouls,
And they did fight with queafinefs, conftrain'd,

As

As men drink potions, that their weapons only
Seem'd on our fide, but for their fpirits and fouls,
This word, rebellion, it had froze them up,
    But now the bifhop,
Turns infurrection to religion ;
Suppos'd fincere and holy in his thoughts,
He's follow'd both with body and with mind,
And doth enlarge his rifing with the blood
Of fair King Richard, fcrap'd from Pomfret ftones ;
Derives from heaven his quarrel and his caufe ;
Tells them, he doth beftride a bleeding land
Gafping for life under great Bolingbroke,
And more, and lefs, do flock to follow him.

Nor can the indecency of a prelate's appearing in arms, and the abufe of an authority derived from the facred function, be more ftrongly arraigned, than in the fpeeches of Weftmorland, and John of Lancafter.

WESTMORLAND.
    Then, my lord,
Unto your grace do I in chief addrefs
The fubftance of my fpeech. If that rebellion
Came like itfelf, in bafe and abject routs,
Led on by bloody youth, goaded with rage,
And countenanc'd by boys and beggary ;
I fay, if damn'd commotion fo appear'd
In his true, native, and moft proper fhape,
You, reverend father, and thefe noble lords,.
Had not been here to drefs the ugly form
Of bafe and bloody infurrection
With your fair honours. You, my lord archbifhop,
Whofe fee is by a civil peace maintain'd,

    Whofe

Whofe beard the filver hand of peace hath touch'd,
Whofe learning and good letters peace hath tutor'd,
Whofe white inveftments figure innnocence,
The dove and very bleffed fpirit of peace ;
Wherefore do you fo ill tranflate yourfelf,
Out of the fpeech of peace, that bears fuch grace,
Into the harfh and boift'rous tongue of war ?

LANCASTER.

My lord of York, it better fhew'd with you,
When that your flock, affembled by the bell,
Encircled you, to hear with reverence
Your expofition on the holy text ;
Than now to fee you here an iron man,
Cheering a rout of rebels with your drum,
Turning the word to fword, and life to death.
That man that fits within a monarch's heart,
And ripens in the fun-fhine of his favour,
Would he abufe the count'nance of the king,
Alack, what mifchiefs might he fet abroach,
In fhadow of fuch greatnefs ?   With you, lord
            bifhop,
It is ev'n fo.   Who hath not heard it fpoken,
How deep you were within the books of heav'n ?
To us, the fpeaker in his parliament,
To us, th' imagin'd voice of heav'n itfelf,
The very opener and intelligencer
Between the grace, the fanctities of heav'n,
And our dull workings : O, who fhall believe
But you mifufe the rev'rence of your place,
Employ the countenance and grace of heav'n,
As a falfe favourite doth his prince's name,
In deeds difhonourable ?   You've taken up,
Under the counterfeited zeal of God,
The fubjects of his fubftitute. my father ;
And both againft the peace of heav'n and him,
Have here up-fwarm'd them.

                        The

The archbiſhop of York, even when he appears an iron man, keeps up the gravity and ſeeming ſanctity of his character, and wears the mitre over his helmet. He is not like Hotſpur, a valiant rebel, full of noble anger and fierce defiance, he ſpeaks like a cool politician to his friends, and like a deep deſigning hypocrite to his enemies, and pretends he is only acting as phyſician to the ſtate.

I have before obſerved, that Shakeſpear had the talents of an orator as much as of a poet; and I believe it will be allowed the ſpeeches of Weſtmorland and Lancaſter are as proper on this occaſion, and the particular circumſtances are as happily touched as they could have been by the moſt judicious orator. I know not that any poet, ancient or modern, has ſhewn ſo perfect a judgment in rhetoric as our countryman. I wiſh he had employed his eloquence too in arraigning the baſeneſs and treachery of John of Lancaſter's conduct, in breaking his covenant with the rebels.

Piſtol is an odd kind of perſonage, intended, I ſuppoſe, to ridicule ſome faſhionable affectation of bombaſt language.

　　　　　When

When fuch characters exift no longer any
where, but in the writings in which they
have been ridiculed, they feem to have
been monfter's of the poet's brain. The
originals loft and the mode forgot, one
can neither praife the imitation, nor laugh
at the ridicule. Comic writers fhould
therefore always exhibit fome characteriftic diftinctions as well as temporary
modes. Juftice Shallow will for ever rank
with certain fpecies of men ; he is like
a well painted portrait in the drefs of his
age. Piftol appears a mere antiquated
habit, fo uncouthly fafhioned, we can
hardly believe it was made for any thing
but a mafquerade frolic. The poets who
mean to pleafe pofterity, fhould therefore
work as painters, not as taylors, and give
us peculiar features rather than fantaftic
habits: but where there is fuch a prodigious variety of well drawn portraits as
in this play, we may excufe one piece of
mere drapery, efpecially when exhibited
to expofe an abfurd and troublefome
fafhion.

Mine hoftefs Quickly is of a fpecies not
extinct. It may be faid, the author there
finks from comedy to farce, but fhe helps
to compleat the character of Falftaffe, and
some

some of the dialogues in which she is engaged, are diverting.   Every scene in
which Doll Tearsheet appears is indecent,
and therefore not only indefensible but in-
excusable.   There are delicacies of decorum in one age unknown to another age,
but whatever is immoral is equally blameable in all ages, and every approach to
obscenity is an offence for which wit cannot atone, nor the barbarity or the corruption of the times excuse.

Having considered the characters of this
piece, I cannot pass over the conduct of it,
without taking notice of the peculiar felicity with which the fable begins to unfold
itself from the very beginning.

The first scenes give the outlines of the
characters, and the argument of the drama.   Where is there an instance of any
opening of a play equal to this? And I
think I did not rashly affert, that it is one
of the most difficult parts of the dramatic art; for that surely may be allowed so,
in which the greatest masters have very
seldom succeeded.   Euripides is not very
happy in this respect.   Iphigenia in Tauris
begins by telling to herself, in a pretty
long soliloquy, who she is, and all that

happened

happened to her at Aulis.   As Ariſtotle
gives this play the higheſt praiſe, we may
be aſſured it did not in any reſpect offend
the Greek taſte : and Boileau not injudi-
ciouſly prefers this ſimple expoſition, deſtitute as it is of any grace, to the perplexed and tedious declamation of the
modern ſtage.

> Que dès les premiers vers l'action préparée,
> Sans peine, du ſujet applaniſſe l'entrée,
> Je me ris d'un acteur, qui lent à s'exprimer,
> De, ce qu'il veut, d'abord ne fait pas m'informer ;
> Et qui, debrouillant mal une pénible intrigue,
> D'un divertiſſement me fait une fatigue.
> J'aimerois mieux encor qu'il déclinât ſon nom,
> Et dît, Je ſuis Oreſte, ou bien Agamemnon :
> Que d'aller par un tas de confuſes merveilles.
> Sans rien dire à l'eſprit etourdir les oreilles.

That the ſimplicity of Euripides is preferable to the perplexity or bombaſt of
Corneille's manner in developing the ſtory
of ſeveral of his tragedies, no perſon of
juſt taſte I believe will diſpute.   The firſt
ſcene of the Cinna has been ridiculed by
Boileau.   That of Sertorius is not very
happy.   His famous play of Rodogune
is opened by two unknown perſons, one
of whom begins,

Enfin ce jour pompeux, cet heureux jour, nous luit ;

and,

and, after *un tas de confuses merveilles* in the moſt wretched verſe, extended to the length of ſeventy lines, when the reader very impatiently expects to be informed of the whole of the narration, ſtops ſhort with theſe words,

Je vous acheverai le reſte une autre fois.

Two brothers united by the moſt tender friendſhip, living in the ſame palace, having been long in love with the ſame princeſs, never have intimated their paſſion to each other, not out of a motive of jealouſy or diſtruſt, but that their confidents may tell it the ſpectator, and make him ſome amends for the abrupt concluſion of the former converſation. However, ſtill the poor ſpectator is much in the dark, till the queen, who is a perfect Machiavel, relates, merely from love of talking, all the murders ſhe has committed, and thoſe ſhe ſtill intends to commit, to her waiting-woman, for whoſe parts ſhe expreſſes at the ſame time a ſovereign contempt.

Here I cannot help taking notice, that as the poet's want of art made it neceſſary to ſet the queen to prate of her former crimes, to let us into the fable ; ſo ignorance of human nature betrayed him, in
a ſuc-

a fucceeding fcene, into the enormous ab-
furdity of making both Rodogune and the
queen, without hefitation, the one advife
the lover to murder his miftrefs, the other
the fon to murder his mother.   Here
again an inftance offers itfelf of our Shakefpear's fuperior knowledge of the heart of
man.   King John wifhes to inftigate Hubert to kill Prince Arthur, but obferve
with what difficulty he exprefles his horrid
purpofe :

King JOHN.

Come hither, Hubert. O my gentle Hubert
We owe thee much ; within this wall of flefh
There is a foul counts thee her creditor,
And with advantage means to pay thy love :
And, my good friend, thy voluntary oath
Lives in this bofom, dearly cherifhed.
Give me thy hand, I had a thing to fay—
But I will fit it with fome better time,
By heaven, Hubert, I'm almoft afhamed
To fay what good refpect I have of thee.

HUBERT,

I am much bounden to your majefty.

King JOHN

Good friend, thou haft no caufe to fay fo yet—
But thou fhalt have—and creep time ne'er fo flow,
Yet it fhall come for me to do thee good.
I had a thing to fay—but let it go :
The fun is in the heav'n, and the proud day,
Attended with the pleafures of the world,
Is all too wanton, and too full of gaudes,

To

To give me audience. If the midnight bell
Did with his iron tongue and brazen mouth
Sound one unto the drowfy race of night ;
If this fame were a church-yard where we ftand,
And thou poffeffed with a thoufand wrongs ;
Or if that furly fpirit melancholy
Had bak'd thy blood and made it heavy-thick,
Which elfe runs tickling up and down the veins,
Making that idiot laughter keep mens eyes,
And ftrain their cheeks to idle merriment ;
(A paffion hateful to my purpofes)
Or if thou could'ft fee me without eyes,
Hear me without thine ears, and make reply
Without a tongue, ufing conceit alone,
Without eyes, ears, and harmful found of words ;
Then, in defpight of broad-ey'd watchful day,
I would unto thy bofom pour my thoughts :
But ah, I will not—yet I love thee well ;
And by my troth, I think, thou lov'ft me well.

O N

ON THE

PRÆTERNATURAL

BEINGS.

The poet's eye, in a fine frenzy rolling,
Doth glance from heav'n to earth, from earth to
     heav'n,
And as imagination bodies forth
The forms of things unknown, the poet's pen
Turns them to ſhape, and gives to airy nothing,
A local habitation and a name.
Midſummer Night's Dream.

ON THE

PRÆTERNATURAL

B Æ I N G S.

AS the genius of Shakefpear, through
the whole extent of the poet's province, is the object of our enquiry, we
fhould do him great injuftice, if we did
not attend to his peculiar felicity, in thofe
fictions and inventions, from which poetry
derives its higheft diftinction, and from
whence it firft affumed its pretenfions to
divine infpiration, and appeared the affo-
ciate of religion.

The ancient poet was admitted into the
fynod of the Gods : he difcourfed of their
natures, he repeated their counfels, and,
without the charge of impiety or prefumption, difclofed their diffenfions, and pub-
lifhed their vices. He peopled the woods
with nymphs, the rivers with deities ; and,
that he might ftill have fome being within
call

call to his affiftance, he placed refponfive echo in the vacant regions of air.

In the infant ages of the world, the credulity of ignorance greedily received every marvellous tale : but, as mankind increafed in knowledge, and a long feries of traditions had eftablifhed a certain mythology and hiftory, the poet was no longer permitted to range, uncontrolled, through the boundlefs dominions of fancy, but became reftrained in fome meafure, to things believed or known.——Though the duty of poetry to pleafe and to furprife ftill fubfifted, the means varied with the ftate of the world, and it foon grew neceffary to make the new inventions lean on the old traditions.—The human mind delights in novelty, and is captivated by the marvellous, But even in fable itfelf requires the credible.—The poet, who can give to fplendid inventions, and to fictions new and bold, the air and authority of reality and truth, is mafter of the genuine fources of the Caftalian fpring, and may juftly be faid to draw his infpiration from *the well-head of a pure poefy*.

Shakefpear faw how ufeful the popular fuperftitions had been to the ancient poets :
he

he felt that they were neceſſary to poetry
itſelf. One needs only to read ſome modern French heroic poems to be convinced how poorly epic poetry ſubſiſts on the
pure elements of hiſtory and philoſophy:
Taſſo, though he had a ſubjeſt ſo popular,
at the time he wrote, as the deliverance of
Jeruſalem, was obliged to employ the operations of magic, and the interpoſition of
angels and dæmons, to give the marvell-
lous, the ſublime, and, I may add, that
religious air to his work, which ennobles
the enthuſiaſm, and ſanctifies the fiction
of the poet. Arioſto's excurſive muſe wan-
ders through the regions of romance, attended by all the ſuperb train of chivalry,
giants, dwarfs, and enchanters, and however theſe poets, by the ſevere and frigid
critics may have been condemned for giving ornaments not purely claſſical, to their
works; I believe every reader of taſte ad-
mires, not only the fertility of their imagination, but the judgment with which they
availed themſelves of the ſuperſtition of the
times, and of the cuſtoms and modes of
the country, in which they laid their
ſcenes of action.

To recur, as the learned ſometimes do,
to the mythology and fables of other ages,
and

and other countries, has ever a poor effect : Jupiter, Minerva, and Apollo, only embellish a modern ftory, as a print from their ftatues adorns the frontifpiece.—We admire indeed the art of the fculptors who give their images with grace and majefty; but no devotion is excited, no enthufiafm kindled, by the reprefentations of characters whofe divinity we do not acknowledge.

When the Pagan temples ceafed to be revered, and the Parnaffian mount exifted no longer, it would have been difficult for the poet of later times to have preferved the divinity of his mufe inviolate, if the weftern world too had not had its facred fables. While there is any national fuperftition which credulity has confecrated, any hallowed tradition long revered by vulgar faith ; to the fanctuary, that afylum, may the poet refort.——Let him tread the holy ground with reverence ; refpect the eftablifhed doctrine; exactly obferve the accuftomed rites, and the attributes of the object of veneration ; then fhall he not vainly invoke an inexorable or abfent deity. Ghofts, fairies, goblins, elves, were as propitious, were as affiftant to Shakefpear, and gave as much of the fublime, and of the marvellous,

to

to his fictions, as nymphs, fatyrs, fawns,
and even the triple Geryon, to the works
of ancient bards. Our poet never carries
his præternatural beings beyond the limits
of the popular tradition. It is true, that
he boldly exerts his poetic genius and fa-
cinating powers in that magic circle, *in*
which none e'er durst walk but he · but as
judicious as bold, he contains himfelf within it. He calls up all the ftately phantoms
in the regions of fuperftition, which our
faith will receive with reverence. He
throws into their manners and language a
myfterious folemnity, favourable to fuperftition in general, with fomething highly
characteriftic of each particular being which
he exhibits. His witches, his ghofts, and
his fairies, feem fpirits of health or goblins damn'd ; *bring with them airs from*
heaven, or blafts from hell. His ghofts are
fullen, melancholy, and terrible. Every
fentence, utter'd by the witches, is a prophecy or a charm ; their manners are malignant, their phrafes ambiguous, their
promifes delufive.——The witches caul-
dron is a horrid collection of what is moft
horrid in their fuppofed incantations. Ariel
is a fpirit, mild, gentle, and fweet, pof-
fefs'd of fupernatural powers, but fubject
to the command of a great magician.

The

The fairies are fportive and gay; the innocent artificers of harmlefs frauds, and mirthful delufions. Puck's enumeration of the feats of a fairy is the moft agreeable recital of their fuppofed gambols.

To all thefe beings our poet has affign-ed tafks, and appropriated manners adapt-ed to their imputed difpofitions and cha-racters; which are continually developing through the whole piece, in a feries of ope-rations conducive to the cataftrophe. They are not brought in as fubordinate or cafu-al agents, but lead the action, and govern the fable; in which refpect our country-man has entered more into theatrical pro-priety than the Greek tragedians.

Every fpecies of poetry has its diftinct duties and obligations. The drama does not, like the epic, admit of epifode, fu-perfluous perfons, or things incredible; for, as it is obferved by a critic of great inge-nuity and tafte, * " that which paffes in " reprefentation, and challenges, as it were, " the fcrutiny of the eye, muft be truth " itfelf, or fomething very nearly ap-" proaching to it." It fhould indeed be what our imagination will adopt, though
our

* Hurd on dramatic Imitation.

our reafon would rejeƈt it.   Great caution
and dexterity are required in the dramatic
poet to give an air of reality to fiƈtitious
exiftence.

In the bold attempt to give to airy nothing a local habitation and a perfon, regard muft be paid to fix it in fuch fcenes,
and to difplay it in fuch aƈtions, as are
agreeable to the popular opinion.——
Witches holding their fabbath, and falut-
ing paffengers on the blafted heath ; ghofts,
at the midnight hour, vifiting the glimpfes
of the moon, and whifpering a bloody fecret, from propriety of place and aƈtion,
derive a credibility very propitious to the
fcheme of the poet. *Reddere perfonæ—
convenientia cuique,* cannot be lefs his duty in regard to thefe fuperior and divine,
than to human charaƈters.   Indeed, from
the invariablenefs of their natures, a greater confiftency and uniformity is neceffary ;
but moft of all, as the belief of their intervention depends entirely on their manners and fentiments fuiting with the pre
conceived opinion of them.

The magician Profpero raifing a ftorm ;
witches performing infernal rites ; or any
other exertion of the fuppofed powers and
                                    qualities

qualities of the agent, were eafily credited by the vulgar.

The genius of Shakefpear informed him that poetic fable muft rife above the fimple tale of the nurfe; therefore he adorns the beldame tradition with flowers gathered on claffic ground, but ftill wifely fuffering thofe fimples of her native foil, to which the eftablifhed fuperftition of her country has attributed a magic fpell, to be predominant. Can any thing be more poetical than Profpero's addrefs to his attendant fpirits before he difmiffes them.

PROSPERO.

Ye elves of hills, brooks, ftanding lakes and groves,
And ye that on the fands with printlefs foot
Do chafe the ebbing Neptune; and do fly him
When he comes back; ye demy-puppets, that,
By the moon-fhine, the green four ringlets make,
Whereof the ewe not bites; and you, whofe paftime
Is to make midnight mufhrooms; that rejoice
To hear the folemn curfew; by whofe aid
(Weak mafters though you be) I have bedimm'd
The noon-tide-fun, call'd forth the mutinous winds,
And 'twixt the green-fea and the azured vault
Set roaring war; to the dread rattling thunder.
Have I given fire, and rifted Jove's ftout oak
With his own bolt: the ftrong-bas'd promontory
Have I made fhake, and by the fpurs pluckt up
The pine and cedar: graves at my command
Have wak'd their fleepers; op'd, and let them forth,
By my fo potent art.

Here

Here are agreeably fummed up the popular ftories concerning the power of magicians. The incantations of the witches in Macbeth are more folemn and terrible than thofe of the Erichtho of Lucan, or of the Canidia of Horace. It may be faid, indeed, that Shakefpear had an advantage derived from the more direful character of his national fuperftitions.

A celebrated writer in his ingenious letters on chivalry, has obferved, that the Gothic manners, and Gothic fuperftitions, are more adapted to the ufes of poetry, than the Grecian. The devotion of thofe times was gloomy and fearful, not being purged of the terrors of the Celtic fables. The prieft often availed himfelf of the dire inventions of his predeceffor, the Druid. The church of Rome adopted many of the Celtic fuperftitions ; others, which were not eftablifhed by it. as points of faith, ftill maintained a traditional authority among the vulgar. Climate, temper, modes of life, and inftitutions of government, feem all to have confpired to make the fuperftitions of the Celtic nations melancholy and terrible. Philofophy had not mitigated the aufterity of ignorant devotion, orrctamed the fierce fpirit of enthufiafm. As the bards, who were our philofophers

G   and

and poets, pretended to be poffeffed of
the dark fecrets of magic and divination,
they certainly encouraged the ignorant credulity, and anxious fears, to which fuch
impoftures owe their fuccefs and credit.
The retired and gloomy fcenes appointed
for the moft folemn rites of devotion ; the aufterity and rigour of druidical difcipline and
jurifdiction ; the fafts, the penances, the fad
excommunications from the comforts and
privileges of civil life ; the dreadful anathe-
ma, whofe vengeance purfued the wretched
beyond the grave which bounds all human
power and moral jurifdiction muft deeply
imprint on the mind all thofe forms of fuperftition fuch an hierarchy prefented. The
bard who was fubfervient to the druid, had
mixed them in his heroic fong ; in his hiftorical annals ; in his medical practice :
genii affifted his heroes ; dæmons decided
the fate of the battle ; and charms cured
the fick, or the wounded. After the confecrated groves were cut down, and the
temples demolifhed, the tales that fprung
from thence were ftill preferved with religious reverence in the minds of the people.

The poet found himfelf happily fituated
amidft enchantments, ghofts, goblins ;
every element fuppofed the refidence of a
kind

kind of deity ; the genius of the mountain, the fpirit of the floods, the oak endued with facred prophecy, made men walk a-broad with a fearful apprehenfion.

Of powers unfeen, and mightier far than they.

On the mountains and in the woods, ftalked the angry fpectre; and in the gayeft and moft pleafing fcenes, even within the cheerful haunts of men, amongft villages and farms,

Tripp'd the light fairies and the dapper elves.

The reader will eafily perceive what refources remained for the poet in this vifionary land of ideal forms. The general fcenery of nature, confidered as inanimate, only adorns the defcriptive part of poetry ; but being, according to the Celtic traditions, animated by a kind of intelligences, the bard could better make ufe of them for his moral purpofes. That awe of the immediate prefence of the deity, which, among the reft of the vulgar, is confined to temples and altars, was here diffufed over every object. They paffed trembling through the woods, and over the mountain, and by the lakes, inhabited by thefe invifible powers ; fuch apprehenfions muft indeed

Deepen the murmur of the falling floods,
And fhed a browner horror on the woods ;

give fearful accents to every whifper of

the

the animate or inanimate creation, and
arm every fhadow with terrors.

With great reafon, therefore it was af-
ferted, that the weftern bards had advantage over Homer in the fuperftitions of
their country. The religious ceremonies
of Greece were more pompous than folemn,
and feemed as much a part of their civil
inftitutions, as belonging to fpiritual matters : nor did they imprefs fo deep a fenfe
of invifible beings, and prepare the mind
to catch the enthufiafm of the poet, and
to receive with veneration the phantoms
he prefented.

Our countryman has another fuperiority over the Greek poets, even the earli-
eft of them, who, having imbibed the
learning of myfterious Egypt, addicted
themfelves to allegory ; but our Gothic
bard employs the potent agency of facred
fable, inftead of mere amufive allegory.
When the world becomes learned and phi-
lofophical, fable refines into allegory. But
the age of fable is the golden age of poetry ; when the beams of unclouded reafon,
and the fteady lamp of inqufitive philofophy throw their penetrating rays upon
the phantoms of imagination, they difcover them to have been mere fhadows,
formed by ignorance. The thunderbolts
of

of Jove, forged in Cimmerian caves ; the
ceſtus of Venus, woven by hands of the
attracting Graces, ceaſe to terrify and al-
lure. Echo, from an amorous nymph,
fades into voice, and nothing more ; the
very threads of Iris's ſcarf are untwiſted ;
all the poet's ſpells are broken, his charms
diſſolved ; deſerted on his own enchanted
ground, he takes refuge in the groves of
philoſophy ; but there his divinities eva-
porate in allegory, in which myſtic and
inſubſtantial ſtate they do but weakly
aſſiſt his operations. By aſſociating his
muſe with philoſophy, he hopes ſhe may
eſtabliſh with the learned the worſhip ſhe
won from the ignorant ; ſo makes her quit
the old traditional fable, from whence ſhe
derived her firſt authority and power, to
follow airy hypotheſis, and chimerical ſyſ-
tems. Allegory, the daughter of fable,
is admired by the faſtidious wit, and ab-
ſtruſe ſcholar, when her mother begins to
be treated as ſuperannuated, fooliſh, and
doting ; but however well ſhe may pleaſe
and amuſe, not being worſhipped as divine, ſhe does not awe and terrify like
ſacred mythology, nor ever can eſtabliſh
the ſame fearful devotion, nor aſſume ſuch
arbitrary power over the mind. Her perſon is not adapted to the ſtage, nor her

qualities

qualities to the bufinefs and end of dramatic reprefentation. L'Abbé du Bos has judicioufly diftinguifhed the reafons why allegory is not fit for the drama. What the
critic inveftigated by art and ftudy, the
wifdom of nature unfolded to our unlettered poet, or he would not have refifted
the prevalent fafhion of his allegorizing
age; efpecially as Spencer's Fairy Queen
was the admired work of the times.

Allegorical beings, performing acts of
chivalry, fell in with the tafte of an age
that affected abftrufe learning, romantic
valour, and high-flown gallantry. Prince
Arthur, the Britifh Hercules, was brought
from ancient ballads and romances, to be
allegorized into the knight of magnanimity, at the Court of Gloriana. His knights
followed him thither, in the fame moraliz-
ed garb, and even the queftynge beaft received no lefs honour and improvement
from the allegorizing art of Spencer, as
has been fhewn by a critic of great learning, ingenuity, and tafte in his obfervations on the Fairy Queen.

Our firft theatrical entertainments, after
we emerged from grofs barbarifm, were
of the allegorical kind. The Chriftmas
carol,

carol, and carnival fhews, the pious paf-
times of our holy-days, were turned into
pageantries and mafques, all fymbolical
and allegorical ——Our ftage rofe from
hymns to the virgin, and encomiums on
the patriarchs and faints : as the Grecian
tragedies from the hymns to Bacchus. Our
early poets added narration and action to
this kind of pfalmody, as Æfchylus had
done to the fong of the goat. Much more
rapid indeed was the progrefs of the Grecian ftage towards perfection.—Philofophy,
poetry, eloquence, all the fine arts, were
in their meridian glory, when the drama
firft began to dawn at Athens, and glori-
oufly it fhone forth, illumined by every
kind of intellectual light.

Shakefpear, in the dark fhades of Gothic barbarifm, had no refources but in
the very phantoms that walked the night
of ignorance and fuperftition : or in touching the latent paffions of civil rage and
difcord; fure to pleafe beft his fierce and
barbarous audience, when he raifed the
bloody ghoft, or reared the warlike ftan-
dard. His choice of thefe fubjects was judicious, if we confider the times in which
he lived; his management of them fo
mafterly

mafterly, that he will be admired in all times.

In the fame age, Ben. Johnfon, more proud of his learning than confident of his genius, was defirous to give a metaphyfi-cal air to his compofitions. He compofed many pieces of the allegorical kind, efta-blifhed on the Grecian mythology, and rendered his play-houfe a perfect panthe-on.—Shakefpear difdained thefe quaint de-vices; an admirable judge of human na-ture, with a capacity moft extenfive, and an invention moft happy, he contented himfelf with giving dramatic manners to hiftory, fublimity and its appropriated powers and charms to fiction; and in both thefe arts he is unequalled.—The Cataline and Sejanus of Johnfon are cold, crude, heavy pieces; turgid where they fhould be great; bombaft where they fhould be fublime; the fentiments extravagant; the manners exaggerated; and the whole un-dramatically conducted by long fenato-rial fpeeches, and flat plagiarifms from Tacitus and Salluft. Such of this author's pieces as he boafts to be *grounded on anti-quity and folid learning, and to lay hold on removed myfteries* *, have neither the ma-jefty

* Prologue to the Mafque of Queens.

jefty of Shakefpec.r's ferious fables. nor the
pleafing fportfulnefs and poetical imagination of his fairy tales. Indéed if we compare our countryman, in this refpeét, with
the moft admired writers of antiquity, we
fhall, perhaps, not finc. him inferior to
them.—Æfchylus, with greater impetuo-
fity of genius than even our countryman,
makes bold incurfions into the blind chaos
of mingled allegory and fable, but he is
not fo happy in diffufing the folemn fhade;
in cafting the dim, religious light that
fhould reign there. When he introduces
his furies, and other fupernatural beings,
he expofes them by too glaring a light ;
caufes affright in the fpeétator, but never
rifes to imparting that unlimited terror
which we feel when Macbeth to his bold
addrefs,

How now ! ye fecret, foul, and midnight hags,.
What is't you do ?

is anfwered,

A deed without a name.

The witches of the foreft are as important in the tragedy of Macbeth, as the
Eumenides in the drama of Æfchylus; but
our poet is infinitely more dexterous and
judicious in the conduét of their part.
The fecret, foul, and midnight hags are
not introduced into the caftle of Macbeth;

G 5   they

they never appear but in their allotted region of folitude and night, nor act beyond their fphere of ambiguous prophecy, and malignant forcery. The Eumenides, fnoring in the temple of Apollo, and then appearing as evidence againft Oreftes in the Areopagus, feem both acting out of their fphere, and below their character. It was the appointed office of the venerable goddeffes, to avenge the crimes unwhipt of juftice, not to demand the public trial of guilty men. They muft lofe much of the fear and reverence in which they were held for their fecret influence of the mind, and the terrors they could inflict on criminal confcience, when they were reprefented as obliged to have recourfe to the ordinary method of revenge, by being witneffes and pleaders in a court of juftice, to obtain the corporal punifhment of the offender. Indeed, it is poffible, that the whole ftory of this play might be allegorical, as thus, that Oreftes, haunted by the terrors which purfue the guilty mind confeffed his crime to the Areopagus, with all the aggravating circumftances remorfe fuggefted to him, from a pious defire to expiate his offence, by fubmitting to whatever fentence this refpectable affembly fhould pronounce for that purpofe. The oracle which commanded

manded him to put Clytemneſtra to death, would plead for him with his judges: their voices being equal for abſolving or puniſhing, wiſdom gives her vote for abſolving him.

Thus conſidered, what appears ſo odd in the mouth of the goddeſs, that ſhe is little affected by the circumſtance of Clytemneſtra's relation to the murderer, becauſe ſhe herſelf had no mother, means only, that juſtice is not governed by any affection or perſonal conſideration, but acts by an invariable and general rule. If the oracle commanded, and the laws juſtified the act of Oreſtes, by appointing the next in blood to avenge the murder, then other circumſtances of a ſpecial and inferior kind, were not to have any weight. I am inclined to think this tragedy is a mixture of hiſtory and allegory. Æſchylus affected the allegorical manner ſo much as to form a tragedy, called the Ballance, upon the allegory in Homer, of Jupiter weighing the fates of Hector and Achilles*; and it is apparent, that the Prometheus of this author, is the ancient allegory of Prometheus wrought into a drama   Prometheus makes his firſt appearance with two ſymbo-

* Apud Plut de modo. leg poetas.

fymbolical perfons, Violence and Force, which are, apparently, of the poet's fiction. Pere Brumoy intimates a fufpicion that this tragedy is an allegory, but imagines it alludes to Xerxes or Darius, becaufe it abounds with reflections on tyranny. To flatter the republican fpirit, all the Grecian tragedies are full of fuch reflections. But an oblique cenfure on the Perfian monarch could not have excufed the direct imputations thrown on the character of Jupiter, if the circumftances of the ftory had been taken in a literal fenfe; nor can it be fuppofed that the Athenians would have endured the moft violent affronts to have been offered to the character of that deity to whom they every day offered facrifice. An allegory being fometimes a mere phyfical hypothefis, without impiety might be treated with freedom.—It is probable that many allegories brought from the hieroglyphic land of Ægypt, were, in the groffer times of Greece, literally underftood by the vulgar; but, in more philofophic ages, were again tranfmuted into allegory; which will account for the mythology of the Greeks and Ægyptians varying greatly, but ftill preferving fuch a refemblance as fhews them to be derived from the fame origin.

Jealous

Jealous of the neighbouring ftates, and ever attentive to the glory and intereft of their commonwealth, an Athenian audience liftened with pleafure to any circumftances, in their theatrical entertainments, which reflected honour on their country. The inftitution of the Areopagus by the exprefs command of Minerva; a perpetual amity promifed by Oreftes between Argos and Athens in the tragedy of the Eumenides; and a prophecy of Prometheus, which threw a luftre on the author of the race of the Heraclidæ, were circumftances, without queftion, feduloufly fought by the poet, and favourably received by the fpectator. But though fuch fubjects might be chofen, or invented, as would introduce fome favourable incidents, or flattering reflections, this intention did not always reign through the whole drama.

It has been juft now obferved, that Shakefpear has an advantage over the Greek poets, in the more folemn, gloomy, and myfterious air of his national fuperftitions; but this avails him only with critics of deep penetration and true tafte, and with whom fentiment has more fway than authority. The learned have received the
popular

popular tales of Greece from their poets;
ours are derived to them from the illiterate
vulgar. The phantom of Darius, in the
tragedy of the Perſians, evoked by ancient
rites, is beheld with reverence by the ſcholar, and endured by the *bel eſprit*. To·
theſe the ghoſt of Hamlet is an object
of contempt or ridicule. Let us candidly
examine theſe royal ſhades, as exhibited to us by theſe great maſters in the
art of exciting pity and terror, Æſchylus
and Shakeſpear; and impartially decide
which poet throws moſt of the ſublime into the præternatural character; and, alſo,
which has the art to render it moſt efficient
in the drama. This enquiry may be more
intereſting, as the French wits have often
mentioned Hamlet's ghoſt as an inſtance
of the barbariſm of our theatre. The Perſians, of Æſchylus, is certainly one of the
moſt auguſt ſpectacles that ever was repreſented on a theatre; nobly imagined, happily ſuſtained, regularly conducted, deeply intereſting to the Athenian people, and
favourable to their great ſcheme of reſiſt-
ing the power of the Perſian monarch. It
would be abſurd to depriciate this excellent piece, or to bring into a general compariſon with it, a drama of ſo different
kind as the tragedy of Hamlet. But it is
                                          ſurely

furely allowable to compare the Perfian
phantom with the Danifh ghoft; and to
examine, whether any thing but prejudice,
in favour of the ancients, protects the fuperftitious circumftances relative to the
one, from the ridicule with which thofe
accompanying the other are treated. Atoffa,
the widow of Darius, relates to the fages
of the Perfian council, a dream and an
omen; they advife her to confult the fhade
of her dead lord, upon what is to be done
in the unfortunate fituation of Xerxes juft
defeated by the Greeks. In the third act
fhe enters offering to the Manes a libati-
on compofed of milk, honey, wine, oil,
&c. upon this Darius iffues from his tomb.
Let the wits, who are fo fmart on our
ghoft's difappearing at the cock's crowing,
explain why, in reafon, a ghoft in Perfia,
or in Greece, fhould be more fond of
milk and honey, than averfe in Denmark,
to the crowing of a cock. Each poet adopted, in his work, the fuperftition relative to his fubject; and the poet who does
fo, underftands his bufinefs much better
than the critic, who, in judging of that
work, refufes it his attention, The phantom of Darius comes forth in his regal
robes to Atoffa and the Satraps in council,
who,

who, in the Eaſtern manner, pay their
ſilent adorations to their emperor. His
quality of ghoſt does not appear to make
any impreſſion upon them ; and the Satraps
ſo exactly preſerve the characters of courtiers, that they do not venture to tell him
the true ſtate of the affairs of his kingdom, and its recent diſgraces : finding he
cannot get any information from them, he
addreſſes himſelf to Atoſſa, who does not
break forth with that paſſion and tenderneſs one ſhould ſuppoſe ſhe would do on
the ſight of her long loſt huſband ; but
very calmly informs him, after ſome flattery on the conſtant proſperity of his reign,
of the calamitous ſtate of Perſia under
Xerxes, who has been ſtimulated by his
courtiers to make war upon Greece.   The
phantom, who was to appear ignorant of
what was paſt, that the Athenian ear
might be ſoothed and flattered with the
detail of their victory at Salamis, is allowed for the ſame reaſon, ſuch preſcience as
to foretell their future triumph at Platea.
Whatever elſe he adds by way of council
or reproof, either in itſelf, or in the mode
of delivering it, is nothing more than
might be expected from any old counſellor
of ſtate.   Darius gives his advice to the
old men, to enjoy whatever they can, becauſe

cauſe riches are of no uſe in the grave. As this touches the moſt abſurd and ridiculous foible in human nature, the increaſe of a greedy and ſolicitous deſire of wealth as the period of enjoyment of it becomes more precarious and ſhort, the admonition has ſomething of a comic and ſatirical turn, unbecoming the ſolemn character of the ſpeaker, and the ſad exigency upon which he was called. The intervention of this præternatural being gives nothing of the marvelous or the ſublime to the piece, nor adds to, or is connected with its intereſt. The ſupernatural diveſted of *the auguſt and the terrible* make but a poor figure in any ſpecies of poetry; uſeleſs and unconnected with the fable, it wants propriety in dramatic poetry. Shakeſpear had ſo juſt a taſte that he never introduced any præternatural character on the ſtage that did not aſſiſt in the conduct of the drama. Indeed he had ſuch a prodigious force of talents he could make every being his fancy created ſubſervient to his deſigns. The uncouth, ungainly monſter Caliban, is ſo ſubject to his genius, as to aſſiſt in bringing things to the propoſed end and perfection. And the ſlight fairies, *weak maſters though they be*, even in their wanton gambols,

bols, and idle sports, perform great tasks
by *his so potent art.*

But to return to the intended comparison
between the Grecian shade and the Danish
ghost. The first propriety in the conduct of
this kind of machinery, seems to be, that
the præternatural person be intimately connected with the fable; that he increase the
interest, add to the solemnity of it, and
that his efficiency, in bringing on the ca-
tastrophe, be in some measure adequate to
the violence done to the ordinary course of
things in his visible interposition. These
are points peculiarly important in dramatic poetry, as has been before observed.
To these ends it is necessary this being
should be acknowledged and revered by the
national superstition, and every operation
that developes the attributes, which the
vulgar opinion, or nurse's legend, taught
us to ascribe to him, will augment our
pleasure; whether we give the reins to
imagination, and as spectators, willingly
yield ourselves up to the pleasing delusion,
or, as critics, examine the merit of the
composition. I hope it is not dificult to
shew, that in all these capital points our
author has excelled. At the solemn midnight hour, Horatio and Marcellus, the
schoolfellows

fchoolfellows of young Hamlet, come to
the centinels upon guard, excited by a report that the ghoft of their late monarch
had fome preceding nights appeared to
them. Horatio, not being of the credu-
lous vulgar, gives little credit to the ftory,
but bids Bernardo proceed in his relation.

BERNARDO.

Laft night of all,
When yon fame ftar, that's weftward from the pole,
Had made his courfe t'illume that part of heav'n,
Where now it burns, Marcellus and myfelf,
The bell then beating one——

Here enters the ghoft, after you are thus
prepared. There is fomething folemn and
fublime in thus regulating the walking of
the fpirit, by the courfe of the ftar: It
intimates a connection and correfpondence
between things beyond our ken, *and above
the vifible diurnal fphere.* Horatio is affected with that kind of fear which fuch an
appearance would naturally excite. He
trembles, and turns pale. When the violence of the emotion fubfides, he reflects,
that probably this fupernatural event por-
tends fome danger lurking in the ftate.
This fuggeftion gives importance to the
phænomenon, and engages our attention.
Horatio's relation of the king's combat with
the

the Norwegian, and of the forces the young
Fortinbras is affembling in order to attack
Denmark, feems to point out from what
quarter the apprehended peril is to arife.
Such appearances, fays he, preceded the
fall of mighty Julius, and the ruin of the
great commonwealth; and he adds, fuch
have often been the omens of difafters
in our own ftate.   There is great art in this
conduct.   The true caufe of the royal
Dane's difccntent could not be gueffed at :
it was a fecret which could be only reveal-
ed by himfelf.   In the mean time, it was
neceffary to captivate our attention, by
demonftrating, that the poet was not going to exhibit fuch idle and frivolous gambols as ghofts are by the vulgar often reprefented to perform.   The hiftorical teftimony, that, antecedent to the death of
Cæfar,

>   The graves ftood tenantlefs, and the fheeted dead
>   Did fqueak and gibber in the Roman ftreets.

gives credibility and importance to this
phænomenon.   Horatio's addrefs to the
ghoft is brief and pertinent, and the whole
purport of it agreeable to the vulgar conceptions of thefe matters.

>   HORATIO.
>   Stay, illufion !
>   If thou haft any found, or ufe of voice,
>   Speak to me.

                                                      If

If there be any good thing to be done,
That may to thee do eafe, and grace to me,
Speak to me
If thou art privy to thy country's fate,
Which happily foreknowing may avoid,
Oh fpeak !
Or, if thou haft uphoarded in thy life
Extorted treafure in the womb of earth,
For which they fay, you fpirits oft walk in death,
Speak of it.

Its vanifhing at the crowing of the cock is another circumftance of the eftablifhed fu-perftition.

Young Hamlet's indignation at his mo-ther's hafty and inceftuous marriage, his forrow for his father's death, his character of that prince, prepare the fpectator to fympathize with his wrongs and fufferings. The fon, as is natural, with much more vehement emotion than Horatio did, ad-dreffes his fathers fhade. Hamlet's ter-ror, his aftonifhment, his vehement de-fire to know the caufe of this vifitation, are irrefiftibly communicated to the fpec-tator by the following fpeech.

HAMLET.
Angels and minifters of grace defend us !
Be thou a fpirit of health, or goblin damn'd,
Bring with thee airs from heaven, or blafts from
    hell,
Be thy intents wicked or charitable,

Thou

Thou com'ſt in ſuch a queſtionable ſhape,
That I will ſpeak to thee. I'll call thee Hamlet,
King, father, royal Dane : oh! anſwer me ;
Let me not burſt in ignorance ; but tell,
Why thy canonized bones,' hearſed in death,
Have burſt their cearments ? Why the ſepulchre,
Wherein we ſaw thee quietly in-urn'd,
Hath op'd his ponderous and marble jaws,
To caſt thee up again ? What may this mean,
That thou, dead corſe, again, in compleat ſteel,
Reviſit'ſt thus the glimpſes of the moon,
Making night hideous !

Never did the Grecian muſe of tragedy
relate a tale ſo full of pity and terror as is
imparted by the ghoſt. Every circum
ſtance melts us with compaſſion ; and with
what horror do we hear him ſay !

GHOST.
But that I am forbid
To tell the ſecrets of my priſon-houſe,
I could a tale unfold ; whoſe lighteſt word
Would harrow up thy ſoul, freeze thy young blood,
Make thy two eyes, like ſtars, ſtart from their
ſpheres,
Thy knotted and combined locks to part,
And each particular hair to ſtand on end
Like quills upon the fretful porcupine :
But this eternal blazon muſt not be
To ears of fleſh and blood.

All that follows is ſolemn, ſad, and deeply
affecting.

Whatever

Whatever in Hamlet belongs to the præternatural is perfectly fine; the reſt of the play does not come within the ſubject of this chapter.

The ingenious criticiſm on the play of the Tempeſt, publiſhed in the Adventurer, has made it unneceſſary to enlarge on that admirable piece, which alone would prove our author to have had a fertile, a ſublime, and original genius.

THE

THE

TRAGEDY

OF

MACBETH.

H

THE

TRAGEDY

OF

MACBETH.

THIS piece is perhaps one of the greatest exertions of the tragic and poetic powers, that any age or any country has produced. Here are opened new sources of terror, new creations of fancy. The agency of witches and spirits excites a species of terror, that cannot be effected by the operation of human agency, or by any form or disposition of human things. For the known limits of their powers and capacities, set certain bounds to our apprehensions; mysterious horrors, undefined terrors, are raised by the intervention of beings whose nature we do not understand, whose actions we cannot controul,

H 2 and

and whofe influence we know not how to
efcape. Here we feel through all the faculties of the foul, and to the utmoft extent of her capacity. The apprehenfion
of the interpofition of fuch agents, is the
moft falutary of all fears. It keeps up in
our minds a fenfe of our connection with
awful and invifible fpirits, to whom our
moft fecret actions are apparent, and from
whofe chaftifement innocence alone can
defend us. From many dangers power
will protect; many crimes may be concealed by art and hypocrify; but when
fupernatural beings arife, to reveal, and to
revenge, guilt blufhes through her mafk,
and trembles behind her bulwarks.

Shakefpear has been fufficiently juftified
by the beft critics, for availing himfelf of
the popular faith in witchcraft; and he is
certainly as defenfible in this point, as
Euripides and other Greek tragedians, for
introducing Jupiter, Diana, Minerva, &c.
whofe perfonal intervention, in the events
exhibited on the ftage, had not obtained
more credit with the thinking and philo-
fophical part of their fpectators than tales·
of witchcraft had done among the wife
and learned here. Much later than the
age in which Macbeth lived, even in
Shake-

Shakefpear's own time, there were fevere
ftatutes extant againft witchcraft.

Some objections have been made to the
Hecate of the Greeks, being joined to the
witches of our country.

Milton, a more correct writer, has often
mixed the Pagan deities even with the
moft facred characters of our religion.
Our witches power was fuppofed to be
exerted only in little and low mifchief :
this therefore being the only inftance where
their interpofition is recorded in the revolutions of a kingdom, the poet thought,
perhaps that the ftory would pafs off better, with the learned at leaft, if he added
the celebrated Hecate to the weird fifters;
and fhe is introduced, chiding their prefumption, for trading in prophecies and
affairs of death.   The dexterity is admirable with which the predictions of the
witches (as Macbeth obferves) prove true
to the ear, but falfe to the hope, according to the general condition of vain ora-
cles.   With great judgment the poet has
given to Macbeth the very temper to be
wrought upon by fuch fuggeftion.   The
bad man is his own tempter.   Richard
III. had a heart that prompted him to do

H 3   all

all that the worſt demon could have ſuggeſted, ſo that the witches had been only
an idle wonder in this ſtory ; nor did he
want ſuch a counſellor as Lady Macbeth ;
a ready inſtrument like Buckingham, to
adopt his projects, and execute his orders,
was ſufficient. But Macbeth, of a generous diſpoſition, and good propenſities,
but with vehement paſſions and aſpiring
wiſhes, was a ſubject liable to be ſeduced
by ſplendid proſpects, and ambitious counſels. This appears from the following
character given of him by his wife:

> Yet do I fear thy nature ;
> It is too full o'th' milk of human kindneſs
> To catch the neareſt way.   Thou wouldſt be
>   great ;
> Art not without ambition ; but without
> The illneſs ſhould attend it.   What thou wouldſt
>   highly,
> That wouldſt thou holily ; wouldſt not play falſe,
> And yet wouldſt wrongly win.

So much inherent ambition in a character,
without other vice, and full of the milk of
human kindneſs, though obnoxious to
temptation, yet would have great ſtruggles
before it yielded, and as violent fits of
ſubſequent remorſe.

If the mind is to be medicated by the
operations of pity and terror, ſurely no
means

means are so well adapted to that end, as
a strong and lively reprefentation of the
agonizing ftruggles that precede, and the
terrible horrors that follow wicked actions.
Other poets thought they had fufficiently
attended to the moral purpofe of the drama, in making the furies purfue the per-
petrated crime. Our author waves their
bloody daggers in the road to guilt, and
demonftrates, that as foon as a man begins to hearken to ill fuggeftions, terrors
environ, and fears diftract him. Tendernefs and conjugal love combat in the
breafts of a Medea and a Herod in their
purpofed vengeance. Perfonal affection
often weeps on the theatre, while jealoufy
or revenge whet the bloody knife ; but
Macbeth's emotions are the ftruggles of
confcience; his agonies are the agonies of
remorfe. They are leffons of juftice, and
warnings to innocence. I do not know
that any dramatic writer, except Shakefpear, has fet forth the pangs of guilt fe-
parate from the fear of punifhment. Cly-
temneftra is reprefented by Euripides as
under great terrors, on account of the
murder of Agamemnon ; but they arife
from fear, not repentance. It is not the
memory of the affaffinated hufband which
haunts and terrifies her, but an apprehen-

fion

fion of vengeance from his furviving fon :
when fhe is told Oreftes is dead, her mind
is again at eafe.   It muft be allowed, that
on the Grecian ftage, it is the office of
the chorus to moralize, and to point out,
on every occafion, the advantages of virtue over vice.   But how much lefs affecting are their animadverfions than the teftimony of the perfon concerned ! Whatever belongs to the part of the chorus has
hardly the force of dramatic imitation.
The chorus is in a manner without perfonal character or intereft, and no way an
agent in the drama.   We cannot fympathize with the cool reflections of thefe idle
fpectators, as we do with the fentiments
of the perfons in whofe circumftances and
fituation we are interefted.

The heart of man, like iron and other
metal, is hard, and of firm refiftance,
when cold, but, warmed, it becomes mal-
leable and ductile.   It is by touching the
paffions and exciting fympathetic emotions, not by fentences, that the tragedian
muft make his impreffions on the fpectator.   I will appeal to any perfon of tafte,
whether the following fpeeches of Wolfey,
in another play of Shakefpear, the firft a
foliloquy, the fecond addreffed to his fervant

vant Cromwell, in which he gives the tes-
timony of his experience, and the result
of his own feelings, would make the same
impreſſion, if uttered by a ſet of ſpecula-
tive ſages in the epiſode of a chorus.

WOLSEY.

So farewell to the little good you bear me !
Farewell, a long farewell to my greatneſs !
This is the ſtate of man ; to-day he puts forth
The tender leaves of hopes, to-morrow bloſſoms,
And bears his bluſhing honours thick upon him,
The third day comes a froſt, a killing froſt,
And when he thinks, good eaſy man, full ſurely
His greatneſs is a ripening, nips his root ;
And then he falls, as I do. I have ventur'd,
Like little wanton boys, that ſwim on bladders,
Theſe many ſummers in a ſea of glory,
But far beyond my depth ; my high-blown pride
At length broke under me, and now has left me,.
Weary and old with ſervice, to the mercy
Of a rude ſtream, that muſt for ever hide me.
Vain pomp and glory of this world, I hate ye ;
I feel my heart new open'd. Oh, how wretched
Is that poor man, that hangs on princes' favours !
There is, betwixt the ſmile we would aſpire to,
That ſweet aſpect of princes, and our ruin,
More pangs and fears than war or women have :
And when he falls, he falls like Lucifer,
Never to hope again.

And in another place,

Let's dry our eyes, and thus far hear me, Cromwel! ;
And when I am forgotten, as I ſhall be,
And ſleep in dull cold marble, where no mention

H 5

Of me muft more be heard, fay then, I taught
    thee,
Say, Wolfey, that once trod the ways of glory,
And founded all the depths and fhoals of honour,
Found thee a way, out of his wreck, to rife in ;
A fure and fafe one, though thy mafter mifs'd it.
Mark but my fall, and that which ruin'd me ;
Cromwell, I charge thee, fling away ambition,
By that fin fell the angels ; how can man then,
The image of his maker, hope to win by't ?
Love thyfelf laft ; cherifh thofe hearts that hate
    thee ;
Corruption wins not more than honefty.
Still in thy right hand carry gentle peace,
To filence envious tongues, be juft. and fear not.
Let all the ends thou aim'ft at, be thy country's,
Thy god's, and truth's ; then if thou fall'ft, O
    Cromwell,
Thou fall'ft a bleffed martyr.   Serve the king ;
And—pr'ythee, lead me in ;
There take an inventory of all I have,
To the laft penny, 'tis the king's.   My robe,
And my integrity to heav'n, is all
I dare now call mine own.   O Cromwell, Crom-
    well,
Had I but ferv'd my God with half the zeal
I ferv'd my king, he would not in mine age
Have left me naked to mine enemies.

    I felected thefe two paffages as contain-
ing reflections of fuch a general kind, as
might be with leaft impropriety tranf-
feired to the chorus; but if even thefe
would lofe much of their force and pathos
if not fpoken by the fallen ftatefman, how
                much

much more would thofe do, which are the
expreffions of fome inftantaneous emotion,
occafioned by the peculiar fituation of the
perfon by whom they are uttered! The
felf-condemnation of a murderer makes a
very deep impreffion upon us when we are
told by Macbeth himfelf that hearing,
while he was killing Duncan, one of the
grooms cry God blefs us, and Amen the
other, he durft not fay, Amen. Had a
formal chorus obferved that a man in fuch
a guilty moment durft not implore that
mercy of which he ftood moft in need, it
would have had but a flight effect. All
know the deteftation with which virtuous
men behold a bad action. A much more
falutary admonition is given when we are
fhewn he terrors that are combined with
guilt in the breaft of the offender.

Our author has fo tempered the confti-
tutional character of Macbeth, by infufing
into it the milk of human kindnefs, and a
ftrong tincture of honour, as to make the
moft violent perturbation, and pungent
remorfe, naturally attend on thofe fteps to
which he is led by the force of temptation.
Here we muft commend the poet's judgment, and his invariable attention to confiftency of character; but more amazing
is

is the art with which he exhibits the movement of the human mind, and renders
audible the filent march of thought : traces
its modes of operation in the courfe of
deliberating, the paufes of hefitation, and
the final act of decifion : fhews how reafon
checks, and how the paffions impel ; and
difplays to us the trepidations that precede, and the horrors that purfue acts of
blood. No fpecies of dialogue but that
which a man holds with himfelf, could
effect this. The foliloquy has been permitted to all dramatic writers ; but its true
ufe has been underftood only by our author, who alone has attained to a juft
imitation of nature in this kind of felf-
conference.

It is certain men do not tell themfelves
who they are, and whence they came ;
they neither narrate nor declaim in the
folitude of the clofet, as Greek and French
writers reprefent. Here then is added to
the drama, an imitation of the moft difficult and delicate kind, that of reprefent-
ing the internal procefs of the mind in rea-
foning and reflecting ; and it is not only
a difficult, but very ufeful art, as it beft
affifts the poet to expofe the anguifh of
remorfe, to repeat every whifper of the
internal

internal monitor, confcience, and, upon
occafion, to lend her a voice *to amaze the
guilty and appal the free.* As a man is a-
verfe to expofe his crimes, and difcover the
turpitude of his actions, even to the faithful friend and trufty confident, it is more
natural for him to breathe in foliloquy the
dark and heavy fecrets of the foul, than
to utter them to the moft intimate affo-
ciate. The conflicts in the bofom of Macbeth, before he committed the murder,
could not, by any other means, have been
fo weil expofed. He entertains the prophecy of his future greatnefs with com-
placency, but the very idea of the means
by which he is to attain it fhocks him to
the higheft degree.

> This fupernatural folliciting
> Cannot be ill ; cannot be good. If ill,
> Why hath it giv'n me the earneft of fuccefs,
> Commencing in a truth ? I'm Thane of Cawdor.
> If good, why do I yield to that fuggeftion,
> Whofe horrid image doth unfix my hair,
> And make my feated heart knock at my ribs.
> Againft the ufe of nature ?

There is an obfcurity and ftiffnefs in part
of thefe foliloquies, which I wifh I could
charge entirely to the confufion of Macbeth's mind, from the horror he feels at
the thought of the murder; but our author is too much addicted to the obfcure
bom-

bombaft, much affected by all forts of
writers in that age. The abhorrence
Macbeth feels at the fuggeftion of affafi-
nating his k:ng, brings him back to this
determination,

> If chance will have me king, why, chance may
>   crown me
> Without my ftir.

After a paufe, in which we may fuppofe
the ambitious defire of a crown to return,
fo far as to make him undetermined what
he fhall do, and leave the decifion to future time and unborn events, he con-
cludes,

> Come what come may,
> Time and the hour runs thro' the rougheft day.

By which, I confefs, I do not with his two
laft commentators imagine is meant either
the tautology of time and the hour, or an
allufion to time painted with an hour-
glafs, or an exhortation to time to haften
forward, but rather to fay *tempus & hora*,
time and occafion, will carry the thing
through, and bring it to fome determined
point and end, let its nature be what it
will. In the next foliloquy he agitates
this great queftion concerning the propofed murder. One argument againft it, is,
that fuch deeds muft. be fupported by
others of like nature.

But,

But, in thefe cafes,
We ftill have judgment here ; that we but teach
Bloody inftructions, which, being taught, return
To plague th' inventor ; this even-handed juftice
Commends th' ingredients of our poifon'd chalice
To our own lips

He proceeds next to confider the peculiar relations in which he ftands to Duncan.

He's here in double truft :
Firft, as I am his kinfman and his fubject,
Strong both againft the deed ; then, as his hoft,
Who fhould againft his murd'rer fhut the door ;
Not bear the knife myfelf.

Then follow his arguments againft the deed, from the admirable qualities of the king.

Befides, this Duncan
Hath borne his faculties fo meekly, hath been
So clear in his great office, that his virtues
Will plead, like angels, trumpet-tongu'd again
The deep damnation of his taking off.

So, fays he, with many reafons to dif-fuade, I have none to urge me to this act, but a vaulting ambition ; which by a daring leap, often procures itfelf a fall. And thus having determined, he tells Lady Macbeth,

We will proceed no further in this bufinefs.
He hath honour'd me of late ; and I have bought
Golden opinions from all forts of people,
Which would be worn, now in their neweft glofs,
Not caft afide fo foon.

Mac-

Macbeth, in debating with himfelf, chiefly dwells upon the guilt, and touches
fomething on the danger of affaflinating
the king.   When he argues with Lady
Macbeth, knowing her too wicked to be
affected by the one, and too daring to be
deterred by the other, he urges, with great
propriety, what he thinks may have more
weight with one of her difpofition ; the
favour he is in with the king, and the
efteem he has lately acquired of the people.   In anfwer to her charge of cowardice, he finely diftinguifhes between manly courage and brutal ferocity.

MACBETH.

I dare do all that may become a man ;
Who dares do more, is none.

At length, overcome, rather than perfuaded, he determines on the bloody deed.

I am fettled, and bend up
Each corp'ral agent to this terrible feat

How terrible to him, how repugnant to
his nature, we plainly perceive, when,
even in the moment that he fummons up
the refolution needful to perform it, horrid phantafms prefent themfelves ; murder alarmed by his centinel ; the wolf
ftealing towards his defign ; witchcraft ce-
lebrating pale Hecate's offerings ; the
mid-

midnight ravifher invading fleeping innocence, feem his affociates; and bloody
daggers lead him to the very chamber of
the king.   At his return from thence, his
fenfe of the crime he has committed, appears fuitable to the repugnance he had to
undertake it.   He tells Lady Macbeth,
that, of the grooms who flept in Duncan's
chamber,

MACBETH.

There's one did laugh in's fleep, and one cry'd
    Murder !
They wak'd each other ; and I ftood and heard
    them ;
But they did fay their prayers, and addrefs them
Again to fleep.

LADY.

There are two lodg'd together.

MACBETH.

One cry'd, God blefs us ! and, Amen ! the other !
As they had feen me with thefe hangman's hands.
Liftening their fear, I could not fay, Amen !
When they did fay, God blefs us !

LADY.

Confider it not fo deeply.

MACBETH.

But wherefore could I not pronounce, Amen ?
I had moft need of blefling, and Amen
Stuck in my throat.

MACBETH.

Methought, I heard a voice cry, Sleep no more !
Macbeth doth murder fleep ; the innocent fleep.

Then

Then he replies, when his lady bids him
carry back the daggers;

MACBETH.

> I'll go no more.
> I am afraid to think what I have done ;
> Look on't again I dare not.

How natural is the exclamation of a person, who, from the fearlefs ftate of un-
fufpecting innocence, is fallen into the
fufpicious condition of guilt, when, upon
hearing a knocking at the gate, he cries
out,

MACBETH.

> How is it with me, when every noife appals me ?

The poet has contrived to throw a
tincture of remorfe even into Macbeth's
refolution to murder Banquo.—He does
not proceed in it like a man, who, impeni-
tent in crimes, and wanton in fuccefs, gaily
goes forward in his violent career ; but
feems impelled on, and ftimulated to this
additional villainy, by an apprehenfion.
that, if Banquo's pofterity fhould inherit
the crown, he has facrificed his virtue, and
defiled his own foul in vain.

MACBETH.

> If 'tis fo,
> For Banquo's iffue have I 'filed my mind,
> For them, the gracious Duncan have I murder'd ;
>   Put

Put rancours in the veſſel of my peace
Only for them ; and my eternal jewel
Given to the common enemy of man,
To make them kings, the ſeed of Banquo kings

His deſire to keep Lady Macbeth innocent
of his intended murder, and yet from the
fullneſs of a throbbing heart, uttering what
may render ſuſpected the very thing he
wiſhes to conceal, ſhews how deeply the
author enters into human nature in general, and in every circumſtance preſerves
the conſiſtency of the character he exhibits.

How ſtrongly is expreſſed the great truth,
that to a man of courage, the moſt terrible
object is the perſon he has injured, in the
following addreſs to Banquo's ghoſt :

MACBETH.

What man dare, I dare.
Approach thou like the rugged Ruſſian bear,
The arm'd rhinoceros, or Hyrcan tyger,
Take any ſhape but that, and my firm nerves
Shall never tremble ; or, be alive again,
And dare me to the deſart with thy ſword ;
If trembling I evade it, then proteſt me
The baby of a girl. Hence, terrible ſhadow !
Unreal mock'ry hence !

It is impoſſible not to ſympathize with the
terrors

terrors Macbeth expreffes in his difordered
fpeech.

MACBETH.

It will have blood——They fay, blood will have
    blood.
Stones have been known to move, and trees to
    fpeak ;
Augurs, that underftand relations, have,
By magpies, and by coughs, and rooks, brought
    forth
The fcret'ft man of blood.

The perturbation with which Macbeth
again reforts to the witches, and the tone
of refentment and abhorrence with which
he addreffes them, rather expreffes his
fenfe of the crimes to which their promifes
excited him, than any fatisfaction in the
regal condition thofe crimes had procured.

MACBETH.

How now you fecret, black, and midnight hags !
What is't you do ?

The unhappy and difconfolate ftate of
the moft triumphant villainy, from a con-
fcioufnefs of the internal deteftation of
mankind to that flagitious greatnefs to
which they are forced to pay external ho-
mage is finely expreffed in the following
words :

MACBETH.

MACBETH.

I have liv'd long enough: my way of life
Is fall'n into the fear, the yellow leaf :
And that which fhould accompany old age,
As honour, love, obedience, troops of friends,
I muft not look to have ; but in their ftead,
Curfes the loud but deep, mouth-honour,
      breath,
Which the poor heart would fain deny, and dare
      not.

Towards the conclufion of the piece his
mind feems to fink under its load of guilt !
Defpair and Melancholy hang on his words !
We fee his griefs that prefs harder on
him than his enemies, by his addrefs to
the phyfician :

MACBETH.

Can'ft thou not minifter to a mind difeas'd ;
Pluck from the memory a rooted forrow ;
Raze out the written troubles of the brain ;
And with fome fweet oblivious antidote,
Cleanfe the ftuff'd bofom of that perilous ftuff
Which weighs up the heart ?

The alacrity with which he attacks young
Siward, and his reluctance to engage with
Macduff, of whofe blood he fays he has
already had too much, compleat a character which is uniformly preferved from the
opening of the fable, to its conclufion.—
We find him ever anfwering to the firft
idea we were made to conceive of him.

The

The man of honour pierces through the traytor and the affaffin. His mind lofes its tranquillity by guilt, but never its fortitude in danger. His crimes prefented to him, even in the unreal mockery of a vifion, or the harmlefs form of fleeping innocence, terrify him more than all his foes in arms.—It has been very juftly obferved by a late commentator, that this piece does not abound with thofe nice difcriminations of character, ufual in the plays of our author, the events being too great to admit the influence of particular difpofitions. It appears to me, that the character of Macbeth was alfo reprefented lefs particular and fpecial, that his example might be of more univerfal utility. He has therefore placed him on that line on which the major part of mankind may be ranked, juft between the extremes of good and bad; a ftation affailable by various temptations, and which ftands in the need of the guard of cautionary admonition. The fupernatural agents, in fome meafure take off our attention from the other characters, efpecially as they are, throughout the piece, what they have a right to be, predominant in the events. They fhould not interfere but to weave the fatal web, or to unravel it;
they

they ought ever to be the regents of the fable and artificers of the cataſtrophe, as the witches are in this piece.   To preſerve in Macbeth a juſt conſiſtency of character ; to repreſent that character naturally ſuſceptible of thoſe deſires that were to be communicated to it ; to render it intereſting to the ſpectator by ſome amiable qualities; to make it exemplify the dangers of ambition, and the terrors of remorſe ; was all that could be required of the tragedian and the moraliſt.   With all the powers of poetry he elevates a legendary tale, without carrying it beyond the limits of vulgar faith and tradition.   The ſolemn character of the infernal rites would be very ſtriking, if the ſcene was not made ludicrous by a mob of old women, which the players have added to the three weird ſiſters.—The incantation is ſo conſonant to the doctrine of enchantments, and receives ſuch power by the help of thoſe potent miniſters of direful ſuperſtition, the terrible and the miſterious, that it has not the air of poetical fiction ſo much as of a diſcovery of magical ſecrets; and thus it ſeizes the heart of the ignorant, and communicates an irreſiſtible horror to the imagination of even the more informed ſpectator.

Shakeſpear

Shakefpear was too well read in human nature, not to know, that, though reafon may expel the fuperftitions of the nurfery, the imagination does not fo entirely free itfelf from their dominion, as not to re-admit them, if occafion reprefents them, in the very fhape in which they were once revered. The firft fcene in which the witches appear, is not fo happily executed as the others. He has too exactly followed the vulgar reports of the Lapland witches, of whom our failors ufed to imagine they could purchafe a fair wind.

The choice of a ftory, that at once corroborated King James's doctrine of dæmonology, and fhewed the long deftination of his family to the throne of Great Britain, was not lefs polite flattery to his majefty, than Virgil ufes to Auguftus and to the Roman people, in making Anchifes fhew to Æneas the reprefentation of unborn heroes, that were to adorn his line, and augment the glory of their commonwealth. It is reported, that a french wit often laughs at the tragedy of Macbeth for having a legion of ghofts in it. One fhould imagine he either had not learnt Englifh, or had forgot his Latin; for the

fpirits

spirits of Banquo's line are no more ghosts
than the reprefentations of the Julian race
in the Æneid; and there is no ghoft but
Banquo's in the whole play. Euripides,
in the moft philofophic and polite age of
the Athenians, brings the fhade of Poly-
dorus, Priam's fon, upon the ftage, to tell
a very long and lamentable tale. Here is
therefore produced, by each tragedian,
the departed fpirit walking this upper
world for caufes admitted by popular faith.
Among the ancients, the unburied, and
with us the murdered, were fuppofed to do
fo. The apparitions are therefore equally juftifiable or blamable ; fo the laurel
crown muft be adjudged to the poet who
throws moft of the fublime and the marvellous into the fupernatural agent ; beft
preferves the credibility of its intervention, and renders it moft ufeful in the drama. There furely can be no difpute of
the fuperiority of our countryman in thefe
articles. There are many bombaft fpeeches in the tragedy of Macbeth; and thefe
are the lawful prize of the critic : but envy, not content to nibble at faults, ftrikes
at its true object, the prime excellencies
and perfections of the thing it would de-
preciate. One fhould not wonder if a fchool-
boy critic, who neither knows what were

I   the

the superstitions of former times, or the
poet's privileges in all times, should flourish away, with all the rash dexterity of
wit, upon the appearance of a ghost; but
it is strange a man of universal learning,
a real and just connoisseur, and a true genius, should cite, as improper and absurd,
what has been practised by the most celebrated artists in the dramatic way, when
such machinery was authorised by the belief of the people. Is there not reason to
suspect from such uncandid treatment of
our poet by this critic, that he

> Views him with jealous, yet with scornful eyes,
> And hates for arts that caus'd himself to rise ?

The difference between a mind naturally
prone to evil, and a frail one warped by
force of temptations, is delicately distin-
guished in Macbeth and his wife. There
are also some touches of the pencil that
mark the male and female character. When
they deliberate on the murder of the king,
the duties of host and subject strongly plead
with him against the deed. She passes over
these considerations; goes to Duncan's
chamber resolved to kill him, but could
not do it, because, she says, he resembled
her father while he slept. There is some-
thing feminine in this, and perfectly agreeable

able to the nature of the fex ; who, even
when void of principle, are feldom entirely divefted of fentiment ; and thus the
poet, who, to ufe his own phrafe, had
overftepped the modefty of nature in the
exaggerated fiercenefs of her character,
returns back to the line and limits of humanity, and that very judicioufly, by a
fudden impreffion, which has only an inftantaneous effect. Thus fhe may relapfe
into her former wickednefs, and, from the
fame fufceptibility, by the force of other
impreffions, be afterwards driven to dif-
traction. As her character was not compofed of thofe gentle elements out of which
regular repentance could be formed, it
was well judged to throw her mind into
the chaos of madnefs ; and, as fhe had exhibited wickednefs in its higheft degree of
ferocity and atrociousnefs, fhe fhould be
an example of the wildeft agonies of remorfe. As Shakefpear could moft exactly delineate the human mind in its regular
ftate of reafon, fo no one ever fo happily
caught its varying forms in the wanderings
of delirium.

The fcene in which Macduff is informed of the murder of his wife and children,
is fo celebrated, that it is not neceffary to

enlarge upon its merit. We feel there, how much a juſt imitation of natural ſentiments on ſuch a tender occaſion, is more pathetic than choſen terms and ſtudied phraſes. As in the foregoing chapter I have made ſome obſervations on our author's management of the Præternatural Beings, I forbear to enlarge further on the ſubjeĉt of the witches : that he has kept cloſely to the traditions concerning them, is very fully ſet forth in the notes of a learned commentator on his works.

This piece may certainly be deemed one of the beſt of Shakeſpear's compoſitions, and, though it contains ſome faulty ſpeeches, and one whole ſcene entirely abſurd and improper, which art might have corrected or lopped away ; yet genius, powerful genius only, (wild nature's vigour working at the root!) could have produced ſuch ſtrong and original beauties, and adapted both to the general temper and taſte of the age in which it appeared.

UPON

CINNA

CORNEILLE.

UPON THE

CINNA

OF

CORNEILLE.

THOUGH it is an agreeable tafk, upon the whole, to attempt the vindication of injured fame, the pleafure is much allayed by its being combined with a neceffity to lay open the unfairnefs and errors in the proceedings of which we complain. To defend is pleafant, to accufe is painful ; but we muft prove the injuftice of the fentence, before we can demand to have it repealed. The editor of the late edition of Corneille's works, has given the following preface to the tragedy of Cinna : " Having often heard Corneille " and Shakefpear compared, I thought it " proper to fhew their different manner

I 4   " in

" in fubjects that have a refemblance.   I
" have therefore chofen the firft acts of
" the Death of Cæfar, where there is a
" confpiracy, as in Cinna, and in which
" every thing is relative to the confpiracy
" to the end of the third act.   The rea-
" der may compare the thoughts, the
" ftyle, and the judgment of Shakefpear,
" with the thoughts, the ftyle, and the
" judgment of Corneille.   It belongs to
" the readers of all nations to pronounce
" between the one and the other.   A
" Frenchman or an Englifhman might per-
" haps be fufpected of fome partiality.
" To inftitute this procefs, it was neceffary
" to make an exact tranflation ; what was
" profe in the tragedy of Shakefpear is
" rendered into profe ; what was in blank
" verfe into blank verfe, and almoft verfe
" by verfe ; what is low and familiar is
" tranflated familiarly and low.   The
" tranflator has endeavoured to rife with
" the author when he rifes ; and when he
" is turgid and bombaft, not to be more
" or lefs fo than he. The tranflation given
" here is the moft faithful that can be,
" and the the only faithful one in our lan-
" guage of any author ancient or modern.
" I have but a word to add, which is, that
" blank verfe cofts nothing but the trou-
                                " ble

" ble of dictating; it is not more difficult
" to write than a letter.   If people fhould
" take it into their heads to write trage-
" dies in blank verfe, and to act them on
" our theatre, tragedy is ruined ; take
" away the difficulty and you take away
" the merit."

An Englifh reader will hardly forbear
fmiling at this bold affertion concerning
the facility of writing blank verfe.   It is
indeed no hard matter to write bad verfe
of any kind ; but, as fo few of our poets
have attained to that perfection in it which
Shakefpear and Milton have done, we have
reafon to fuppofe the art to be difficult.
Whatever is well done in poetry or eloquence appears eafy to do.   Theatrical
dialogue being an imitation of difcourfe,
our critics do not require the appearance
of effort and labour, but, on the contrary,
the language of nature, and a juft refemblance to the thing imitated.   Poffibly
there is as much of difficulty in blank verfe
to the poet, as there appears of eafe in it
to the reader.   Like the ceftus of Venus,
formed by the happy fkill of the Graces,
it beft exerts its charms while the artifice
of the texture is partly concealed.   Dry-
den, who brought the art of rhyme to

I 5   great.

great excellence, endeavoured to introduce it on our ftage ; but nature and tafte
revolted againft an imitation of dialogue
in a mode fo entirely different from that
in which men difcourfe. The verfe Mr.
de Voltaire thus condemns is perhaps not
lefs happily adapted than the Iambic to
the dramatic offices. It rifes gracefully into the fublime ; it can flide happily into
the familiar ; haften its career if impelled
by vehemence of paffion ; paufe in the hefitation of doubt ; appear lingering and
languid in dejection and forrow ; is capable of varying its accent, and adapting
its harmony, to the fentiment it fhould
convey, and the paffion it would excite,
with all the power of mufical expreffion.
Even a perfon who did not underftand our
language would find himfelf very differently affected by the following fpeeches in
that metre :

LEAR.

Vengeance ! plague ! death ! confufion !———
Fiery ? what fiery quality ? why, Glo'fter,
I'd fpeak with the Duke of Cornwall, and his wife :
The king would fpeak with Cornwall. The dear
    father
Would with his daughter fpeak, commands her
    fervice :
Are they inform'd of this ? my breath and blood !
Fiery ? the fiery duke ? tell the hot duke that—
                        MACBETH.

MACBETH.

I have lived long enough : my way of life
Is fall'n into the fear, the yellow leaf :
And that which should accompany old age,
As honour, love, obedience, troops of friends.
I muft not look to have ; but in their ftead,
Curfes not loud but deep, mouth-honour, breath,
Which the poor heart would fain deny, and dares
    not.

The charm arifing from the tones of
Englifh blank verfe cannot be felt by a
foreigner, who is fo far from being acquainted with the pronunciation of our
language, that he often miftakes the fignification of the moft common words ; of
which there are many remarkable inftances in this boafted tranflation of Julius
Cæfar ; for he does not know that the
word courfe fignifies method of proceed-
ing, but imagines it means a courfe of
difhes, or a race. Brutus replies to Caffius's propofal to kill Cæfar?

BRUTUS.

Our courfe will feem too bloody, Caius Caffius,
To cut the head off, and then hack the limbs,
Like wrath in death, and envy afterwards :
For Antony is but a limb of Cæfar.

Thus it is tranflated by Mr. dè Voltaire.

BRUTUS.

Cette courfe aux Romains paraitrait trop fanglante ;
                      On

On nous reprocherait la colère & l' envie,
Si nous coupons la tête, & puis hachons les mem-
    bres,
Car Antoine n'eft rien qu'un membre de Cæfar.

The following ingenious note is added
by the tranflator. The word courfe, fays
he, perhaps has an allufion to the Lupercal courfe. It alfo fignifies a fervice of
difhes at table. It is very extraordinary
that a man fhould fet up for a tranflator,
with fo little acquaintance in the language
as not to be able to diftinguifh whether a
a word in a certain period fignifies a race,
a fervice of difhes, or a mode of conduct.
In a piece entitled Guillaume de Vade, and
attributed to Mr. de Voltaire, there is a
blunder of the fame kind. Polonius orders his daughter not to confide in the promifes of Hamlet, who, being heir to the
crown, cannot have liberty of choice in
marriage like a private perfon. He muft
not, fays the old ftatefman, carve for himfelf as vulgar perfons do. The French author tranflates it, he muft not cut his own
victuals; and runs on about morfels, as if
Hamlet's dinner, not his marriage, had
been the fubject of debate. The tranflator knew not that the word carve is often
ufed metaphorically in our language for a
                                    perfon's

perfon's framing or fafhioning his lot or portion. We fay, the lover feeds on hope ; the warrior thirfts for glory : would it be fair to tranflate that the lover eats a morfel of hope, and the warrior defires to drink a draught of glory ? If fuch tranflations are allowed, the works of the moft correct author may be rendered ridiculous. It is apparent that Mr. de Voltaire has depended entirely on the affiftance of a dictionary to enable him *to give the moft faithful tranflation that can be, and the only faithful one, in the French language, of any author, ancient or modern.*

It is neceffary to prefent to thofe readers who do not underftand French, the miferable miftakes and galamatheus of this dictionary work. Brutus, in his foliloquy meditating on what Caffius had been urging concerning Cæfar, thus expreffes his apprehenfion, that imperial power may change the conduct of the man.

BRUTUS.
        'Tis a common proof,
That lowlinefs is young ambitions ladder,
Whereto the climber upwards turns his face ;
But when he once attains the utmoft round,
He then unto the ladder turns his back,
Looks in the clouds, fcorning the bafe degrees
By which he did afcend.   So Cæfar may.
                                        Thus

Thus Mr. Voltaire tranflates it,

BRUTUS.
——On fait affez quelle eft l' ambition.
L' échelle des grandeurs à fes yeux fe préfente ;
Elle y monte en cachant fon front aux fpeEtateurs ;
Et quand elle eft haut, alors elle fe montre ;
Alors jufques au ciel élevant fes regards,
D'un coup d'œil meprifant fa vanité dédaigne
Les premiers échelons qui firent fa grandeur.
C'eft ce que peut Cælar.

"One knows what ambition is ; the ladder of grandeurs prefents itfelf to her; in
going up fhe hides her face from the fpectators ; when fhe is at the top then fhe
fhews herfelf ; then rifing her view to the
heavens, with a fcornful look her vanity
difdains the fteps of the ladder that made
her greatnefs.   This it is that Cæfar may
do."

In the original, lowlinefs is young ambition's ladder ; the man who by feign'd
humility, and courtefy, has attained to
the power to which he afpired, turns his
back on thofe humble means by which he
afcended to it ; the metaphor agreeing
both to the man who has gained the top of
the ladder, or to him who has rifen to the
fummit of power.   In the tranflation, ambition afcends by fteps of grandeurs, hid-
ing her face from the fpeEtators, when fhe
is

is at the top, with a look or glance of her eye her vanity difdains the firft fteps fhe took ; which fteps obferve were grandeurs ; fo the allegory is, vanity and ambition difdaining grandeur ; and the image prefented is a woman climbing up a ladder, which is not a very common object, but more fo than vanity's difdaining grandeurs.

I am forry the tranflator had not a better Englifh Dictionary, for on that, not on his own knowledge of our tongue, it is plain he depended. In another inftance it mifleads him. After Portia had importuned Brutus to communicate to her the fecret caufe of his perturbation, he fays to her,

> BRUTUS.
> Porcia, go in a while,
> And, by and by, thy bofom fhall partake
> The fecrets of my heart.
> All my engagements I will conftrue to thee,
> All the charactary of my fad brows.—
> Leave me with hafte.

The dictionary was confulted for the word conftrue ; and thus, according to the ufual form, one may fuppofe it to have ftood : To conftrue, to interpret. This not ferving the purpofe to interpret was
next

next fought; there he finds, to interpret or
to explain; again with indefatigable in-
duſtry, excited by a deſire to excel all
tranſlators and tranſlations, he has recourſe
to the article to explain; under this head
he finds, to unfold or clear up; ſo away
goes the tranſlator to clear up the countenance of Brutus.

> Va, mes ſourcils froncés prennent un air plus doux.

" Go;" ſays he; " my frowning brow ſhall
take a ſofter air."

There are ſo many groſs blunders in this
work it would be tedious to point them out;
but it is to be hoped they will deter other
beaux eſprits from attempting to hurt
works of genius by the maſked battery of
an unfair tranſlation. Mr. Voltaire deſires
that by his tranſlation all Europe will compare the thoughts, the ſtile, and the judgment of Shakeſpear, with the thoughts,
the ſtile, and the judgment of Corneille.
It is difficult, perhaps impoſſible, to make
the graces of ſtyle paſs from one language
to another; and our blank verſe cannot
be equalled by French blank verſe. The
thoughts might in ſome meaſure have been
given, if the tranſlator had underſtood the
words in which Shakeſpear had expreſſed
them.

them. Upon the judgement of the authors in the choice of the ſtory, in the
conduct of it, in exciting the ſympathies
belonging to it, in the faſhioning of the
characters, in the noblenefs of ſentiment,
and the repreſentation of Roman manners, we ſhall upon cloſe examination of
the Cinna and Julius Cæſar be able to pronounce.

As the ſubject of the drama is built on
a conſpiracy which every one is aſſured
had not any effect, and the author has ſo
conducted it as to render the pardon Auguſtus gives the conſpirators an act of political prudence, rather than generous clemency, there is not any thing to intereſt
us but the characters of Cinna, Emilia,
and Maximus. Let us examine how far
they are worthy to do ſo as ſet forth in this
piece ; for we have no hiſtorical acquaintance with them. Emilia is the daughter
of Toranius the tutor of Auguſtus, who
was proſcribed by him in his triumvirate.
As we have not any knowledge of this
Toranius, we are no more concerned about
any cruelty committed upon him than upon any other man, ſo we are not prepared
to enter into the outragious reſentment of
Emilia, eſpecially as we ſee her in the court
of

of Auguſtus under the ſacred relation of
his adopted daughter, enjoying all the privileges of that diſtinguiſhed ſituation, and
treated with the tenderneſs of· paternal
love. Nothing ſo much deforms the feminine character as ferocity of ſentiment.
Nothing ſo deeply ſtains the human character as ingratitude.

This lady, however odious ſhe appears
to the ſpectator, is made to engage Cinna
her lover, who is a nephew of the great
Pompey, in a conſpiracy againſt Auguſtus,
Shakeſpear moſt judiciouſly labour·d to
ſhew that Brutus's motives to kill Cæſar
were perfectly generous and purely-pub-
lic ſpirited. Corneille has not kindled Cinna to his enterprize with any ſpaik of Roman fire. In every thing he appears
treacherous, baſe, and timid. Maximus,
the other conſpirator, ſeems at firſt a better character; but in the third act he makes
a moſt lamentable confeſſion to a ſlave, of
his love for Emilia, and his jealouſy of Cinna: this ſlave gives ſuch advice as one
might expect from ſuch a councellor; he
urges him to betray his aſſociates, and by
means of a lie, to prevail upon Emilia to
go off with him. Thus Maximus becomes
as treacherous and baſe as Cinna his friend,
and

and Emilia his miſtreſs The poet follows
Seneca's account of this affair in making
Livia (who has no other buſineſs in the
drama) adviſe Auguſtus to try the effect
of meaſures of clemency, as his puniſh-
ment of former conſpiracies excited new
ones. Auguſtus tells her ſhe talks like a
woman, treats her counſel with ſcorn, and
then follows it. Auguſtus appears with
dignity and ſenſe in the other ſcene, and
is the only perſon in the play for whom
one has any reſpect. This is the plan of a
work which is to ſhew Corneille's genius
and judgment ſuperior to Shakeſpear's.
As Mr. Voltaire has given his tranſlation of
Julius Cæſar, I will juſt preſent to the reader a literal tranſlation of the firſt ſcene of
the firſt act, which begins by a ſoliloquy.

CINNA, TRAGEDIE.

ACTE PREMIER. SCENE PREMIERE,

EMILIE

Impatiens déſirs d'une illuſtre vengeance,
Dont la mort de mon pere a formé la naiſſance,
Enfans impetueux de mon reſſentiment,
Que ma douleur ſeduite embraſſe aveuglement,
Vous prenez ſur mon ame un trop puiſſant empire.
Durant quelques momens ſouffrez que je reſpire,
Et que je conſidere, en l'etat où je ſuis,
Et ce que je hazarde, & ce que je pourſuis.

Quand

Quand je regarde Augufte au milieu de fa gloire,
Et que vous reprochez à ma trifte mémoire
Que par fa propre main mon père maffacré
Du trône où je le vois fait le premier degré :
Quand vous me prefentez cette fanglante image,
La caufe de ma haine, & l'effet de fa rage,
Je m'abandonne toute à vos ardens tranfports,
Et crois pour une mort lui devoir mille morts.
Au milieu toutefois d'une fureur fi jufte,
J'aime encor plus Cinna que je ne haïs Augufte ;
Et je fens refroidir ce bouillant mouvement,
Quand il faut pour le fuivre expofer mon amant.
Oui, Cinna, contre moi-même je m irrite,
Quand je fonge aux dangers où je te precipite
Quoique pour me fervir tu n'apprehendes rien,
Te demander du fang, c'eft expofer le tien.
D'une fi haute place on n'abat point de tête
Sans attirer fur foi mille & mile tempêtes ;
L'iffue en eft douteufe, & le peril certain.
Un ami deloyal peut trahir ton deffein ;
L'ordre mal concerté, l'occafion mal prife,
Peuvent fur fon auteur renverfer l'enterprife,
Tourner fur tois les coups dont tu le veux frapper;
Dans fa ruine même il peut t'enveloper ;
Et quoi qu'en ma faveur ton amour exécute,
Il te peut en tombant écrafer fous fa chute,
Ah ! ceffe de courir à ce mortel danger :
Te perdre enme vengeant ce n'eft pas me venger.
Un cœur eft trop cruel quand il trouve des charmes
Aux douceurs que corrompt l'amertume des larmes ;
Et l'on doit mettre au rang des plus cuifans mal-
　　heurs
La mort d'un ennemi qui coute tant de pleurs.

　　Mais peut-on en verfer alors qu'on venge un
　　pere ?
Eft-il perte à ce prix qui ne femble légére?

　　　　　　　　　　　　　　　　Et

Et quand fon affaffin tombe fous notre effort,
Doit on confiderer ce que coûte fa mort ?
Ceffez, vaines frayeurs, ceffez, lâches tendreffes,
De jetter dans mon cœur vos indignes faibleffes ;
Et toi qui les produis par tes foins fuperflus,
Amour, fers mon devoir, & ne le combats plus.
Lui ceder c'eft ta gloire, & le vaincre ta honte ;
Montre-toi genereux, fouffrant qu'il te furmonte.
Plus tu lui donneras, plus il te va donner,
Et ne triomphera que pour te couronner.

I do not pretend, as Mr. Voltaire does,
to make the reader a judge of the ftile
of Corneille by my tranflation ; he muft allow for the want of verfification, and be
content with the thoughts, the fentiments,
the conceits of the original.

EMILIA.

" Impatient defires of an illuftrious vengeance, to which the death of my father
gave birth, impetuous children of my refentment, which my deluded forrow em-
braces too blindly, you affume too great
an empire over my mind. Suffer me to
breathe a moment, and let me confider
the ftate I am in, what I hazard, and what
I would attempt. When I behold Cæfar
in the midft of glory, you (I fuppofe this
means, you, the impetuous children of the
impatient defires of an illuftrious vengeance,

geance) reproach my melancholy memory that my father, maſſacred by his hand, was the firſt ſtep to the throne on which I ſee him. And when you preſent me that bloody image, the cauſe of my hatred, the effect of his rage, I abandon myſelf to your violent tranſports, and think that for one death I owe him a thouſand deaths. In the midſt of ſo juſt an indignation I ſtill love Cinna more than I hate Auguſtus; and I find this boiling anger cool, when to obey it I muſt hazard my lover. Yes, Cinna, againſt myſelf, myſelf am angry, when I think of the dangers into which I precipitate thee. Though to ſerve me thou feareſt nothing, to aſk thee for blood is to expoſe thine. One beats not down heads from ſo high a place without drawing upon one's ſelf a thouſand and a thouſand ſtorms; the iſſue is doubtful, the peril is certain. The order ill concerted, the opportunity ill choſen, may on their author overturn the whole enterprize, turn on thee the blow thou wouldſt ſtrike, and even envelope thee in his ruin; and what thou executeſt for my ſake may cruſh thee in its fall. Ah! do not run into this danger. To ruin yourſelf in revenging me is not to revenge me. That heart is too cruel which finds a ſweet-
neſs

nefs in that vengeance which is corrupted
by the bitternefs of forrow ; and one fhould
put in the rank of the greateft misfortunes
the death of an enemy which cofts fo many tears. But can one fhed tears when
one revenges a father? Is there a lofs which
does not feem light at that price ? And
when his affaffin dies by our means, ought
we to confider what his death cofts us?
Ceafe vain fears, ceafe foolifh tendernefs to
affect my heart with your unworthy weak-
neffes: and thou who produceft them by
thy fuperfluous anxieties, O love, affift my
duty, do not combat with it; to yield to
it is thy glory, to vanquifh it thy difgrace;
fhew thyfelf generous, fuffer it to overcome thee. The more thou giveft to it,
the more it will give thee, and will triumph only to crown thee."

> Such mighty nothings in fo ftrange a ftile
> Amaze th' unlearn'd, and make the learned fmile.

The fecond fcene of Emilia, and Fulvia her friend, is not fo abfurd as the foliloquy ; but the anfwer Emilla gives to
Fulvia, who urges to her, that the benefits fhe had received from Auguftus and
the credit fhe has with him fhould miti
gate her refentment, fhews her difpofition
to be ungrateful, violent, and treacherous.

EMILIE.

EMILIE.

Les bienfaits ne font pas toûjours ce que tu penfes ;
D'une main odieufe ils tiennent lieu d'offenfes :
Plus nous en prodiguons à qui nous peut hair,
Plus d'armes nous donnons à qui nous veut trahir.
Il m'en fait chaque jour fans changer mon courage.
Je fuis ce que j'etais, & je puis davantage ;
Et des mêmes préfens qu'il verfe dans mes mains
J'achette contre lui les efprits des Romains.
Je recevrais de lui la place de Livie,
Comme un moyen plus fur d'attenter à fa vie.

" Benefits do not always do what you
think.   From an odious hand they are fo
many offences: the more we beftow upon
thofe who hate us, the more arms we fur-
nifh to thofe who may betray us.   He be-
ftows them upon me every day without
changing my refolution. I am what I was,
and I am able to effect more ; and with
the prefents he pours into my hands I purchafe the hearts of Romans to fet them
againft him.   I would receive from him
the place of Livia, to gain furer means
to attempt his life."

The next fcene Cinna enters, and tells
his furious charmer, that the confpirators
enter into the plot with as much zeal as if
they too were ferving a miftrefs.

CINNA.

Tous s'y montrent portés avec tant d'allegreffe,
Qu'ils femblent comme moi fervir une maîtreffe.—
                                        Plût

Plût aux dieux que vous-même euffiez vû de
    quel zéle
Cette troupe entreprend une action fi belle !
Au feul nom de Céfar, d'Augufte, d'Empereur,
Vous euffiez vû leurs yeux s'enflammer de fureur ;
Et dans un même inftant, par un effet contraire,
Leur front pâlir d'horreur, & rougir de colere.

Here is a childifh play upon words, and
a mere rant : for in thofe times neither the
names of Cæfar, Auguftus, or Emperor
were detefted ; the monfters that afterwards
affumed them might become odious.

The fcene is very long as we may fuppofe where fuch different fentiments and
paffions are to be expreffed as thofe which
belong to the lover and confpirator. Cinna
affures Emilia that he concealed from his
affociates, that to avenge her father and
obtain her he entered into this confpiracy.

CINNA.
Rien n'eft pour vous à craindre ; aucun de nos
    amis
Ne fait ni vos deffeins, ni ce qui m'eft promis :
Et leur parlant tantôt des miferes Romaines,
Je leur ai tû la mort qui fait naître nos haines,
De peur que mon ardeur touchant vos intérêts
D'un fi parfait amour ne trahît les fecrets.

" There is nothing for you to fear;
none of our friends know the defigns, nor

K   what

what is promifed me. In fpeaking of
the miferies of the Romans I was filent
about the death which is the caufe of
our hatred, left my warmth for your interefts fhould betray the fecrets of fuch a
perfect love."

There was not only difcretion but good
fenfe in this, for the fecrets *d'un parfait
amour* might not have been duly attended
to or properly reverenced, by a furly band
of confpirators met to concert meafures for
fuch a perilous enterprize. In the next
fcene Auguftus fends for Cinna and Maximus, to advife with them whether he fhall
reftore liberty to the commonwealth. Here
we have fome refpite from the ftrange med-
ley of tender love and dire revenge, and in
lieu of it a long political difcuffion of the
conveniences and inconveniencies of different modes of Government.

Corneille has borrowed from Dion Caffius, and transferred to Cinna and Maximus, the fpeeches of Agrippa and Mecenas, when Auguftus confulted them whether he fhould demit his power, and live
a private man, as Sylla had done. Mr. Fe-
nelon has very juftly cenfured, as ill fuiting
that fimplicity of ftyle and manner with
which

which Auguftus expreffed himfelf, the following lines :

AUGUSTE.

Cet empire abfolu fur la terre et fur l'onde,
Ce pouvoir fouverain que j'ai fur tout le monde,
Cette grandeur fans bornes, et cet illuftre rang,
Qui m'a jadis coutê tant de peine et de fang,
Enfin tout ce qu'adore en ma haute fortune
D'un courtifan flateur la prefence importune,
N'eft que de ces beautés dont l'eclat eblouit,
Et qu'on ceffe d'aimer fi-tot qu'on en jouit.

" This abfolute empire over the earth
and ocean, this fovereign power that I
have over the whole world, this greatnefs
without limits, and this illuftrious rank
which has heretofore coft me fo much labour and fo much blood; in fine, all that
the troublefome croud of flattering courtiers adores in my high fortune, is but a
piece of pageantry, whofe luftre dazzles,
and that one ceafes to admire as foon as one
poffeffes it."

Thefe oftentatious expreffions are perfectly ridiculous to thofe who are acquainted with the character of the fpeaker: but
there is another fault much more detri-
mental to the drama, which is the averfion
we conceive at the black treachery of Cinna, who when Auguftus confults him as

K 2   his

his friend, whether he fhall lay down his power, and reftore liberty to the commonwealth, advifes him him not to do it, with a great appearance of perfonal attachment to him, and zeal for his country ; but in reality, that he may not lofe a pretence to facrifice him to the revenge of Emilia. This holds forth Cinna to the fpectator as a perfidious friend, a wicked counfellor, a profligate citizen. A more atrocious conduct was perhaps never afcribed to any character on the ftage, where the guilty perfon was intended to excite indignation and abhorrence ; and is therefore the moft flagrantly abfurd in a cafe where the character is that on which the intereft of the play is to turn.

Auguftus having intimated to Cinna at the conclufion of their conference, that he was willing to give Emilia to him, he begins then to reflect upon his perfidy, and urges to Maximus the remorfe he feels for the intended affaffination. The poet feems to be afraid he has not yet fufficiently difgraced his hero, and therefore makes Maximus reply to him thus :

MAXIME.

Formez vos remors d'une plus jufte caufe,
De vos lâches confeils, qui feuls ont arreté

Le

Le bonheur renaiſſant de notre liberté.
C'eſt vous ſeul aujourd'hui qui nous l'avez ôtée,
De la main de Céſar Brute l eut acceptée,
Et n'eut jamais ſouffert qu'un interet leger
De vengeance ou d'amour l'eût remiſe en danger.

" Derive your remorſe from a juſter
cauſe, from your baſe counſels, which
alone put a ſtop to the felicity of reviving
liberty. 'Tis you alone that have now deprived us of it. From the hand of Cæſar
Brutus would have accepted the liberty of
Rome ; and never, from a paltry intereſt of
love or revenge, would have again put it to
hazard."

As every movement in this play is to turn
on mean and ſelfiſh paſſions, as ſoon as
Maximus apprehends his rival is to receive
Emilia as the reward of his enterprize, he
ſuffers his ſlave to betray the plot to Auguſtus. He then endeavours to perſuade
Emilia to eſcape with him. All this is very
aukwardly conducted.

It is ſtrange that a dramatic writer
ſhould not have ſtudied human nature
enough to perceive, that the only character, which cannot intereſt upon the ſtage,
is that which is mean, low, and contemptible. Great ſpirits, even though of a
bad

bad kind, engage our attention to all their operations, becaufe they are capable of producing great events. We are curious to fee what the audacious villain will dare to do, what the cunning one will contrive ; but when a man is prefented to us as a fcoundrel, *un lache,* we difdain to attend to his actions. Therefore, however well the great fcenes of this play may be written ; confidered fingly, they are very injudicioufly managed. We fhall now fee Cinna appear fo defpicable, that to punifh him would be below the dignity of Auguftus ; and to retain him as a friend, unworthy of any man. Auguftus, informed by the double traitor Maximus, fends for Cinna, and reproaches him with every fpecies of bafe ingratitude, tells him he firft gave him his life, enriched him with the fpoils of Antony, upon every occafion had been profufely liberal and kind to him, preferred his intereft even to thofe who had fought for him, and by whofe blood he had purchafed the empire ; and had admitted him, upon the death of Mecenas, into the firft place in his confidence. Auguftus adds too, that it was by his advice he retained his power ; and after all this, fays he, you would affaffinate me. Cinna does not barely deny the confpiracy, but exclaims,

　　　　　　　　　　　" I, Sir,

" I, Sir, have I fuch a treacherous foul,
" fuch a bafe defign!"

Auguftus cuts him fhort in this difgrace-
ful lie, fhewing him he has full information
of the plot; and very juftly fays, " The
liberty of thy country could not be thy
object, for then thou wouldft not have hin-
dered my reftoring it. Thou muft defign
therefore to reign in my place. Alas!
Rome muft be unhappy indeed, if I were
the only obftacle, and that after my death
it fhould not fall into better hands than
thine. Learn to know what thou art:
defcend into thyfelf: thou art honoured,
praifed, and loved, and all tremble before
thee, fo high have I raifed thy fortune:
but thou wouldft be the pity of thofe who
now envy that fortune, if I abandoned thee
to thy own little merit. Contradict me if
thou canft; tell me what is thy merit,
what are thy virtues, what are thy glorious exploits, what are thofe rare qualities
by which thou could'ft pretend to my favour, what is it raifes thee above the vulgar? My favour is thy only glory; thy power
arifes from it; that alone raifes and fupports
thee; it is that, not thou, which is refpect-
ed: thou haft neither rank nor credit but
what arifes from it; and to let thee fall,

I need

I need only draw back the hand that fupports thee."

Quel etait ton deffein, et que pretendais-tu,
Après m'avoir au temple a tes pieds abattu ?
Affranchir ton pays d'un pouvoir monarchique ?
Si j'ai bien entendu tantôt ta politique,
Son falut deformais depend d'un fouverain,
Qui pour tout conferver tienne tout en fa main ;
Et fi fa liberté te faifait entreprendre,
Tu ne m'euffes jamais empeché de la rendre ;
Tu l'aurais acceptée au nom de tout l'etat,
Sans vouloir l'acquerir par un affaffinat.
Quel etait donc ton but ? d'y regner et ma place ?
D'un etrange malheur fon deftin le menace,
Si pour monter au trône et lui donner la loi,
Tu ne trouves dans Rome autre obftacle que moi;
Si jufques a ce point fon fort eft deplorable,
Que tu fois après moi le plus confiderable
Et que ce grand fardeu de l'empire Romain
Ne puiffe après ma mort tomber mieux qu'en ta
       main.
Apprens à te connaître, et defcens en toi-même.
On t'honore dans Rome, on te courtife, on t'aime ;
Chacun tremble fous toi, chacun t' offre des vœux ;
Ta fortune eft bien haut, tu peux ce que je veux :
Mais tu ferais pitié, même a ceux qu'elle irrite,
Si je t' abandonnais a ton peu de merite.
Ofe me dementir, dis-moi ce que tu vaux,
Conte-moi tes vertus, tes glorieux travaux,
Les rares qualités par ou tu m'as dû plaire,
Et tout ce qui t'eleve au-deffus du vulgaire.
Ma faveur fait ta gloire, & ton pouvoir en vient ;
Elle feule t'eleve, & feule te foutient,
C'eft elle qu'on adore, et non pas ta perfonne,
Tu n'as crèdit ni rang qu'autant qu'elle t'en donne;
Et pour te faire choir je n'aurais aujourd'hui
Qu' a retirer la main qui feule eft ton appui.

                          Emilia

Emilia enters, and behaves with the most insolent pride, undaunted assurance, and unfeeling ingratitude ; and declares to Augustus, that as long as she is handsome enough to get lovers he shall never want enemies. Augustus still adheres to his plan of clemency, (for that too is plan, and the result of prudent deliberation, not of generous magnanimity) he pardons Maximus, forgives Cinna in spite of his unworthiness, and bestows upon him Emilia and the consulship. Emilia is at last mitigated, and modestly tells Augustus that heaven has ordained a change in the commonwealth since it has changed her heart. What is there in all this that can move either pity or terror ? In what is it moral, in what is it interesting, where is it pathetic ?

It is a common error in the plan of Corneille's tragedies, that the interest of the piece turns upon some unknown person, generally a haughty princess ; so that instead of the representation of an important event, and the characters of illustrious persons, the business of the drama is the love-intrigue of a termagant lady, who, if she is a Roman, insults the Barbarians, if she is a Barbarian, braves the Romans,

K 5   and

and even to her lover is infolent and fierce.
Were fuch a perfon to be produced on our
theatre, fhe would be taken for a mad poe-
tefs efcaped from her keepers in Bedlam,
who, fancying herfelf a queen, was rant-
ing and delivering her mandates in rhyme
upon the ftage. All the excufe that can
be made for Corneille in fuch reprefentation, is, that characters like thefe, dignified
indeed with nobler fentiments, were admired in the romances in which the manners of chivalry are exaggerated. By the
inftitutions of chivalry every valiant knight
profeffed a peculiar devotion to the fair fex,
in whofe caufe, as the champion of the de-
fencelefs, and protector of the oppreffed,
he was always ready to take arms. A lady's intereft being often the object, and
fometimes her perfon the prize of a combat, fhe was fuppofed to infpire his courage; and, as he was to be not lefs diftinguifhed for politenefs than valour, he affected an air of fubmiffive obedience,
while fhe, by the courtefy of knighthood,
was allowed to affume a ftile of fuperiority and command. To carry thefe manners
into ancient Greece and Rome, and weave
them into a confpiracy there, betrays want
of judgment. In the ftrain of romance
this drama is carried on. The lady enjoins
her

her lover to kill Auguftus; that adven-
ture atchieved he is to hope for her hand ;
his glory is to be derived from her ac-
knowledging him worthy of it ; fhe is continually exhorting him to deferve the honour of being beloved by her. The fate of
Auguftus, of the Roman empire, all the
duties of the citizen and the friend, are to
depend on her decifion. She fays to Auguftus, when he has difcovered the confpiracy, as a fufficient vindication of her
lover,

> Oui, tout ce qu'il a fait, il l'a fait pour me plaire,
> Et j'en etois, feigneur, la caufe et le falaire.

The author certainly intended to recom-
mend Cinna to his fpectators merely as *a
loyal lover*, according to the phrafe of romance: in every other light he appears
contemptible, and indeed fuffers himfelf to
be ufed with the greateft contempt and
indignity. As Shakefpear laboured to fhew
that the motives of Brutus were untinctur-
ed by any bad paffion : on the contrary
every movement in the mind of Cinna has
the character of bafenefs, and whether he
confpires or whether he repents of it, he is
ftill, as he acknowledges himfelf to be,

> Un efprit malheureux,
> Qui ne forme qu'en lache un deffein genereux.

From

From this unhappy wretch who bafely conceives a generous defign, let us turn to Brutus.   There we fhall fee the different judgment and genius of the artifts.   Brutus and Cinna are drawn in the fame fituation, confpiring againft the foremoft man of all this world : in the one we have the features and complexion of a villain, in the other the high-finifhed form of a noble patriot.

U P O N

UPON THE

DEATH

OF

JULIUS CÆSAR.

UPON THE

DEATH

O F

JULIUS CÆSAR.

THE tragedies of Cinna, and Julius
Cæfar, are each of them the reprefentation of a confpiracy ; but it cannot be
denied, that our countryman has been by
far more judicious in his choice of the ftory.
An abortive fcheme, in which fome people of obfcure fame were engaged, and
even in whom, as they are reprefented,
the attempt was pardoned, more from contempt of their abilities and power, than
the clemency of the emperor, makes a
poor figure in contraft with that confpiracy, which, formed by the firft characters
in Rome, effected the deftruction of the
greateft man the world ever produced, and

was

was fucceeded by the moft memorable confequences.   Hiftory furnifhes various examples of bafe and treacherous natures,
of diffolute manners, ruined fortunes, and
loft reputations, uniting in horrid affocia-
tion to deftroy their prince.   Ambition
often cuts itfelf a bloody way to greatnefs.
—Exafperated mifery fometimes plunges
its defperate dagger in the breaft of the
oppreffor.   The cabal of a court the mutiny of a camp, the wild zeal of fanatics,
have often produced events of that nature.
But this confpiracy was formed of very different elements.   It was the genius of
Rome, the rights of her coftitution, the
fpirit of her laws, that rofe againft the ambition of Cæfar ; they fteeled the heart,
and whetted the dagger of the mild, the
virtuous, the gentle Brutus, to give the
mortal wound, not to a tyrant, who had
faftened fetters on his fellow-citizens, but
to the conqueror, who had made the
world wear their chains : one empire only
remained unfubjected to them, and that
he was preparing to fubdue.

Can there be a fubject more worthy of
the tragic mufe, than the imitation of an
action fo important in its confequences, and
unparalleled in all its circumftances ? How
is

is our curiofity excited to difcover what
could engage the man of virtue in an enterprize of fuch a terrible kind ; and why,
after its accomplifhment, inftead of being
ftigmatized with the name of confpirator and affaffin, the decrees of an auguft
fenate, the voice of Rome, unite to place
him one of the firft on the roll of patriots ;
and the fucceffor of the murdered Cæfar,
who devoted to deftruction the moft illuftrious men of Rome, durft not offer violation to the ftatue of Brutus !

To obtain, from the Englifh fpectator
the fame reverence for him, it was neceffary we fhould be made to imbibe thofe doc-
trines, and to adopt the opinion by which
he himfelf was actuated.   We muft be in
the very capitol of Rome ; ftand at the
bafe of Pompey's ftatue, furrounded by
the effigies of their patriots ; we muft be
taught to adore the images of Junius Brutus, the Horatii, Decii, Fabii, and all who
had offered dear and bloody facrifice to the
liberty of their country, to fee this action in
the point of view to which it offered itfelf
to the deliberation of Brutus, and by
which it was beheld by thofe who judged
of it when done.   To the very fcene, to
the very time, therefore, does our poet
transport

tranfport us : at Rome we become Romans ; we are affected by their manners ; we are caught by their enthufiafm. But what a variety of imitations were there to be made by the artift to affect this! and who but Shakefpear was capable of fuch a tafk ? A poet of ordinary genius would have endeavoured to intereft us for Brutus, by the means of fome imagined fond mother, or fonder miftrefs. But can a few female tears wipe out the ftains of affaffination ? A bafe confpirator, a vile affaffin, like the wretched Cinna of Corneille, would Brutus have appeared to us, if only the fame feeble arts had been exerted for him. It is for the genuine fon of ancient Rome, the lover of the liberty of his country, we are interefted. A concern raifed for him, from compaffion to any other perfon, would only have excited fome painful emotions in the fpectator, arifing from difcordant fentiments. Indeed the common aim of tragedy writers feems to be merely to make us uneafy, for fome reafon or other, during the drama. They take any thing to be a tragedy in which there are great perfons, and much lamentation ; but our poet never reprefents an action of one fort, and raifes emotions and paffions of another fort. He excites the fympathies, and the concern

cern, proper to the ſtory. The paſſion of
love, or maternal affeƈtion, may give good
ſubjeƈts for a tragedy. In the fables of
Phædra and Merope thoſe ſentiments belong to the aƈtion ; but they had no ſhare
in the reſolution taken to kill Cæſar ; and,
if they are made to interfere, they adul-
terate the imitation ; if to predominate,
they ſpoil it. Our author diſdains the le-
gerdemain trick of ſubſtituting one paſſion
for another. He is the great magician
that can call forth paſſions of any ſort. If
they are ſuch as time has deſtroyed, or
cuſtom extinguiſhed, he ſummons from
the dead thoſe ſouls in which they once
exiſted. Havcing ſufficiently enlarged on
the general ſcope of our author in this
play, we will now conſider it in the detail.

The firſt ſcene is in the ſtreets of Rome.
The tribunes chide the people for gather-
ing together to do honour to Cæſar's triumph. As certain decorums did not employ the attention of the writers of Shakeſpear's days, he ſuffers ſome poor mechanics to be too loquacious. As it was his
buſineſs to depreſs the charaƈter of Cæſar,
and render his viƈtory over his illuſtrious
rival as odious as poſſible, he judiciouſly
makes

makes one of the tribunes thus addrefs himfelf to the people;

MARULLUS.

Wherefore rejoice ? What conquefts brings he
    home ?
What tributaries follow him to Rome,
To grace in captive bonds his chariot wheels ?
You blocks, you ftones, you worfe than fenfelefs
    things !
O you hard hearts ! you cruel men of Rome !
Knew you not Pompey ? Many a time and oft
Have ye climb'd up to walls and battlements,
To towers and windows, yea, to chimney-tops,
Your infants in your arms, and there have fat
The live-long day with patient expectation,
To fee great Pompey pafs the ftreets of Rome ;
And when you faw his chariot but appear,
Have you not made an univerfal fhout,
That Tyber trembled underneath his banks
To hear the replication of your founds,
Made in his concave fhores ?
And do you now put on your beft attire ?
And do you now cull out an holiday ?
And do you now ftrew flowers in his way,
That comes in triumph over Pompey's blood ?
Be gone———
Run to your houfes, fall upon your knees,
Pray to the gods, to intermit the plague
That needs muft light on this ingratitude.

The next fpeech fhews the general apprehenfion of Cæfar's affuming too great
a degree of power.

FLAVIUS.

         Let no images
Be hung with Cæfar's trophies. I'll about,
And drive away the vulgar from the ftreets ·

                        So

So do you too, where you perceive them thick.
Thefe growing feathers, pluckt from Cæfar's wing,
Will make him fly an ordinary pitch ;
Who elfe would foar above the view of men,
And keeps us all in fervile fearfulnefs.

The fecond fcene is the courfe at the Lupercal games, in which Antony appears the humble courtier of Cæfar. A footh-fayer bids him beware the ides of March.

In the third fcene there is a dialogue between Brutus and Caffius, in which the latter tenderly reproaches Brutus that his countenance is not fo open and cordial to him as formerly ; to this the other replies, he has fome inward difcontent,

And that poor Brutus, with himfelf at war,
Forgets the fhews of love to other men.

This intimation of difcontent encourages Caffius to try to incenfe Brutus againft the growing power of Cæfar. On the fhouts of the mob, Brutus exprefles a fear that they are making Cæfar king, this encourages Caffius to proceed in his defign. He makes two fpeeches, in which he appears envious and malignant to Cæfar, of whom he fpeaks as men do, who, unwilling to confefs the qualities that give to a rival fuperiority, dwell with the malice on petty circumftances,

cumftances, in which he is not diftinguifhed from ordinary men. The French critic is much offended at this fcene, and
fays, it is not in the ftyle of great men.
The language of envy is always low. The
fpeeches of Caffius exprefs well his envious
and peevifh temper, and make him a foil
to fet off to advantage the more noble
mind of Brutus. Caffius endeavours to
ftimulate Brutus to oppofe the encroach-
ments of Cæfar on the liberty of Rome, by
fetting before him its firft deliverer, the
great Junius Brutus; a name revered by
every Roman, but, undoubtedly, adored
by his defcendants.

This is truly imitation, when the poet
gives us the juft copies of all circumftances
that accompanied the action he reprefents.
Corneille's dramas are fantaftic compofitions, void of hiftorical truth, imitation of
character, or reprefentation of manners.
Some few lines from Seneca, ingrafted into
the Cinna, have given it reputation. For,
however cuftom may have taught a very
ingenious and polite people to endure the
infipid fcenes of *l'amoureux et l'amoureufe*,
the fault has been in the poets, not the
fpectators: all their critics have ftrongly
condemned this mode of writing; and the
public,

public, by its approbation of this piece on
account of the scenes between Auguſtus
and Cinna, ſhews plainly how much dialogues of a noble and manly kind would
pleaſe.   Unhappily, Seneca's Auguſtus
makes the Cinna of Corneille appear too
mean and little.   Theſe borrowed ornaments never will aſſort perfectly well with
the piece; they break in upon the harmony of ſentiment, and the proportion of
characters, and fall greatly ſhort of the
eaſy propriety, and becoming grace, of a
perfect ſet of imitations deſigned for, and
fitted to the work, as in this tragedy of
Julius Cæſar, where all characters appear
in due degrees of ſubordination to the
hero of the piece.   Our poet, to intereſt us the more for Brutus, takes every
occaſion to make Caſſius a foil for him.   In
the next ſcene he is repreſented by Cæſar
in an unamiable light; the opportunity of
ſo fit an occaſion is taken, to make ſome
fine reflections on the malignant and envious nature of men, not ſoftened by the
joys of mirth, and endearing intercourſe of
ſocial pleaſures.

CÆSAR. *(To* ANTONY, *apart.)*

Let me have men about me that are fat,
Sleek-headed men, and ſuch as ſleep a-nights:
Yon Caſſius has a lean and hungry look ;
He thinks too much.   Such men are dangerous.

ANTONY

ANTONY.

Fear him not, Cæfar, he's not dangerous ;
He is a noble Roman, and well given.

CÆSAR.

Would he were fatter. But I fear him not :
Yet if my name were liable to fear,
I do not know the man I fhould avoid,
So foon as that fpare Caffius. He reads much ;
He is a great obferver ; and he looks
Quite through the deeds of men. He loves no plays,
As thou doft, Antony ; he hears no mufic ;
Seldom he fmiles, and fmiles in fuch a fort,
As if he mock'd himfelf, and fcorn'd his fpirit,
That could be mov'd to fmile at any thing.
Such men as he be never at heart's eafe
Whilft they behold a greater than themfelves ;
And therefore are they very dangerous.

Cafca's blunt recital of the offer of a
crown to Cæfar, in the next fcene, is much
cenfured by the critic, accuftomed to the
decorums of the French theatre. It is not
improbable the poet might have in his eye
fome perfon of eminence in his days, who
was diftinguifhed by fuch manners. Many
allufions and imitations which pleafe at the
time, are loft to pofterity, unlefs they point
at tranfactions and perfons of the firft con-
fequence. Whether we approve fuch a
character on the ftage or not, we muft allow his narration reprefents the defigns of
Cæfar's party, and the averfion of the Roman people to that royalty to which he
afpired ;

afpired ; and it was right to avoid engaging
the parties in more deep difcourfe, as
Shakefpear intended, by a fort of hiftorical procefs, to fhew how Brutus was led on
to that act to which his nature was averfe.

The firft fcene of the fecond act prefents
Brutus debating with himfelf upon the
point on which Caffius had been urging
him.   Caffius in his foliloquy, fcene third,
act firft, feemed to intimate, that refentment had a fhare in his defire to take off
Cæfar.   Brutus, on the contrary, informs
us, no perfonal motives fway him, but
fuch as are derived from an hereditary
averfion to tyranny, and the pledge the
virtue of his anceftors had given the commonwealth, that a Brutus would not fuffer a king in Rome; and thefe confidera-
tions compel him to take the following refolution :

BRUTUS.
It muft be by his death ; and, for my part,
I know no perfonal caufe to fpurn at him ;
But for the general. He would be crown'd ;
How that might change his nature, there's the
            queftion.
It is the bright day that brings forth the adder ;
And that craves wary walking : Crown him--that--
And then I grant we put a fting in him,
That at his will he may do danger with.
Th' abufe of greatnefs is, when it disjoins
Remorfe from power : and to fpeak truth of Cæfar,
            L   I have

I have not known when his affections sway'd
More than his reason.   But 'tis a common proof,
That lowliness is young ambition's ladder,
Whereto the climber upwards turns his face ;
But when he once attains the upmost round,
He then unto the ladder turns his back,
Looks in the clouds, scorning the base degrees
By which he did ascend.   So Cæsar may :
Then, lest he may, prevent.

How averse he is to the means by which
he is to deliver his country from the danger apprehended, appears in the following
words :

BRUTUS.
Since Cassius first did whet me against Cæsar,
I have not slept.
Between the acting of a dreadful thing,
And the first motion, all the interim is
Like a phantasma, or an hideous dream :
The genius, and the mortal instruments,
Are then in council ; and the state of man,
Like to a little kingdom, suffers then
The nature of an insurrection.

Disguise and concealment are so abhorrent
to the open ingenuity of his nature, that
righteous as he thinks the cause in which
he is going to engage, on hearing his
friends are come to him muffled up at midnight, he cannot help breaking out in the
following manner.

BRUTUS.
O Conspiracy !
Sham'st thou to shew thy dang'rous brow by night,
When

When evils are moſt free ? O then, by day
Where wilt thou find a cavern dark enough.
To maſk thy monſtrous viſage ? Seek none, Con-
  ſpiracy,
Hide it in ſmiles of affability ;
For if thou put thy native ſemblance on,
Not Erebus itſelf were dim enough
 To hide thee from prevention.

Brutus riſes far above his friend and aſſo-
ciate Caſſius, when, with a noble diſdain,
he rejects his propoſal of ſwearing to their
reſolution.

BRUTUS.

No, not an oath. If not the face of men,
The ſufferance of our ſouls, the time's abuſe,
If theſe be motives weak, break off betimes,
And ev'ry man hence to his idle bed ;
So let high-ſighted tyranny range on,
'Till each man drop by lottery. But if theſe,
As I am ſure they do, bear fire enough
To kindle cowards, and to ſteel with valour
The melting ſpirits of women ; then, countrymen,
What need we any ſpur, but our own cauſe,
To prick us to redreſs ? what other bond,
Than ſecret Romans, that have ſpoke the word,
And will not palter ? and what other oath,
Than honeſty to honeſty engag'd
That this ſhall be, or we will fall for it ?
Swear prieſts, and cowards, and men cautelous,
Old feeble carrions, and ſuch ſuffering ſouls
That welcome wrongs : unto bad cauſes, ſwear
Such creatures as men doubt ; but do not ſtain
The even virtue of our enterprize,
Nor the inſuppreſſive mettle of our ſpirits,
To think, that or our cauſe, or our performance,
Did need an oath : when every drop of blood
That ev'ry Roman bears, and nobly bears,

L 2

Is

Is guilty of a feveral Baftardy,
If he doth break the fmalleft particle
Of any promife that hath paft from him.

Is it not wonderful to fee a poor player thus
ennoble the fentiments, and give full ex-
panfion to the magnanimity of the man
ftyled the deliverer of Rome?

Mr. Voltaire is fo little fenfible of the
noble delicacy of this fpeech, that he fays
the confpirators are not Romans, but a
parcel of country-fellows of a former age
who confpire in a tippling-houfe.——Surely there is no partiality in faying our author has given Roman fentiments with a
tincture of the Platonic philofophy to Brutus; and, befides thefe more general cha-
racteriftics, has added many nice touches
which fpecify his perfonal qualities.   We
behold on the ftage the Marcus Brutus of
Plutarch rendered more amiable and more
interefting.   A peculiar gentlenefs of manners, and delicacy of mind, diftinguifh
him from all the other confpirators; and
we cannot refufe to concur with the confeffion of his enemies, and the words of
Antony.

ANTONY.
This was the nobleft Roman of them all :
All the confpirators, fave only he,
Did that they did in envy of great Cæfar;

He

He, only in a general honeſt thought,
And common good to all, made one of them.
His life was gentle, and the elements
So mix'd in him, that nature might ſtand up,
And ſay to all the world ; *This was a man !*

The following ſoliloquy prophetic of the
civil war, ſubſequent to the death of Cæſar,
ſpoken by Antony addreſſing himſelf to
the dead body, is ſublime and ſolemn.

ANTONY.

O pardon me, thou bleeding piece of earth,
That I am meek and gentle with theſe butchers.
Thou art the ruins of the nobleſt man,
That ever lived in the tide of times.
Woe to the hand that ſhed this coſtly blood !
Over thy wounds now do I propheſy,
Which like dumb mouths do ope their ruby lips,
To beg the voice and utterance of my tongue,
A curſe ſhall light upon the limbs of men ;
Domeſtic fury and fierce civil ſtrife,
Shall cumber all the parts of Italy ;
Blood and deſtruction ſhall be ſo in uſe,
And dreadful objects ſo familiar,
That mothers ſhall but ſmile, when they behold
Their infants quarter'd with the hands of war :
All pity choak'd with cuſtom of fell deeds ;
And Cæſar's ſpirit raging for revenge,
Wi.h Até by his ſide come hot from hell,
Shall in theſe confines, with a monarch's voice
Cry Havock, and let ſlip the dogs of war.

This ſpeech ſhews the ſecret enmity Antony bears to the conſpirators, and prepares us for the inflammatory oration
which at the obſequies of Cæſar he pro-
nounces

nounces before the people.—I fhall quote
it at length, for as this tragedy has been
brought by Mr. Voltaire into a comparifon with the Cinna of Corneille, and he is
pleafed to call our Englifh piece a monftrous fpectacle, and takes not the leaft
notice of a fpeech which may be confidered as one of the fineft pieces of Rhetoric
that is extant, I am defirous to fet it immediately before the reader, who will hardly find any thing monftrous in its form,
or abfurd in its matter, but quite the re-
verfe. I fuppofe a popular addrefs and
manner, in an oration defigned for the
populace, would be deemed the moft proper by the beft critics in the art of rhetoric.

ANTONY.

Friends, Romans, countrymen, lend me your ears.
I come to bury Cæfar, not to praife him.
The evil, that men do, lives after them,
The good is oft interred with their bones ;
So let it be with Cæfar ! noble Brutus
Hath told you Cæfar was ambitious ;
If it were fo it was a grievous fault,
And grievoufly hath Cæfar anfwer'd it.
Here, under leave of Brutus, and the reft,
For Brutus is an honourable man,
So are they all, all honourable men,
Come I to fpeak in Cæfar's funeral.
He was my friend, faithful and juft to me ;
But Brutus fays, he was ambitious ;
And Brutus is an honourable man.

He

He hath brought many captives home to Rome,
Whofe ranfoms did the general coffers fill ;
Did this in Cæfar feem ambitious ?
When that the poor have cry'd, Cæfar hath wept ;
Ambition fhould be made of fterner ftuff,
Yet Brutus fays, he was ambitious ;
And Brutus is an honourable man.
You all did fee, that, on the Lupercal
I thrice prefented him a kingly crown,
Which he did thrice refufe.   Was this ambition ?
Yet Brutus fays, he was ambitious ;
And, fure he is an honourable man.
I fpeak not, to difprove what Brutus fpoke,
But here I am to fpeak what I do know.
You all did love him once, not without a caufe ;
What caufe with-holds you then to mourn for him ?
O judgment ! thou art fled to brutifh beafts,
And men have loft their reafon.   Bear with me.
My heart is in the coffin there with Cæfar,
And I muft paufe 'till it come back to me.

I PLEBEIAN.

Methinks, there is much reafon in his fayings, &c.

ANTONY.

But yefterday the word of Cæfar might
Have ftood againft the world ; now lies he there,
And none fo poor to do him reverence.
O mafters ! if I were difpos'd to ftir
Your hearts and minds to mutiny and rage,
I fhould do Brutus wrong, and Caffius wrong,
Who, you all know, are honourable men.
I will not do them wrong : I rather chufe
To wrong the dead, to wrong myfelf and you,
Than I will wrong fuch honourable men.
But here's a parchment with the feal of Cæfar,
I found it in his clofet, 'tis his will ;
Let but the commons hear this teftament,

L 4

Which,.

Which, pardon me, I do not mean to read,
And they would go and kiſs dead Cæſar's wounds,
And dip their napkins in his ſacred blood ;
Yea, beg a hair of him for memory,
And dying, mention it within their wills,
Bequeathing it as a rich legacy
Unto their iſſue.

4 PLEBEIAN.

We'll hear the will ; read it, Mark Antony.

ALL.

The will, the will. We will hear Cæſar's will.

ANTONY.

Have patience, gentle friends, I muſt not read it ;
It is not meet you know how Cæſar lov'd you.
You are not wood, you are not ſtones, but men ;
And, being men, hearing the will of Cæſar,
It will inflame you, it will make you mad.
'Tis good you know not, that you were his heirs ;
For if you ſhould, O what would come of it ?

4 PLEBEIAN.

Read the will, we will hear it ; Antony ; &c.

ANTONY.

Will you be patient ? will you ſtay a while ?
I have o'erſhot myſelf, to tell you of it.
I fear I wrong the honourable men,
Whoſe daggers have ſtabb'd Cæſar. I do fear it.

4 PLEBEIAN.

They were traitors, &c.

ANTONY.

You will compel me then to read the will ?
Then make a ring about the corps of Cæſar,
And let me ſhew you him that made the will.
Shall I deſcend ? and will you give me leave ?

ALL.

Come down.

3 PLEBEIAN.

You ſhall have leave.

ANTONY.

ANTONY.

If you have tears, prepare to shed them now.
You all do know this mantle ; I remember
The first time ever Cæsar put it on,
'Twas on a summer's evening in his tent,
That day he overcame the Nervii.
Look! in this place ran Cassius' dagger through ;
See, what a rent the envious Casca made ;
Through this, the well-beloved Brutus stabb'd ;
And as he pluck'd his cursed steel away,
Mark, how the blood of Cæsar follow'd it !
As rushing out of doors to be resolv'd,
If Brutus so unkindly knock'd, or no :
For Brutus, as you know, was Cæsar's angel,
Judge, oh you gods ! how dearly Cæsar lov'd him ;
This was the most unkindest cut of all ;
For when the noble Cæsar saw him stab,
Ingratitude, more strong than traitor's arms,
Quite vanquish'd him ; then burst his mighty heart;
And, in his mantle muffling up his face,
Even at the base of Pompey's statue,
Which all the while ran blood, great Cæsar fell.
O what a fall was there, my countrymen !
Then I, and you, and all of us fell down :
Whilst bloody treason flourish'd over us.
O, now you weep ! and, I perceive you feel
The dint of pity ; these are gracious drops.
Kind souls ! what, weep you when you but behold
Our Cæsar's vesture wounded ? look you here !
Here is himself, marr'd, as you see by traitors.

I PLEBEIAN.

O piteous spectacle !

ANTONY.

Good friends, sweet friends, let me not stir you up
To such a sudden flood of mutiny :
They that have done this deed, are honourable.
What private griefs they have, alas ! I know not,

L 5   That

That made them do it ; they are wife and honour-
 able ;
And will, no doubt, with reafons anfwer you.
I come not, friends, to fteal away your hearts ;
I am no orator, as Brutus is,
But, as you know me all, a plain blunt man,
That love my friend ; and that they know full well,
That give me public leave to fpeak of him ;
For I have neither wit, nor words, nor worth,
Action nor utt'rance, nor the power of fpeech,
To ftir mens blood ; I only fpeak right on,
I tell you that which you yourfelves do know ;
Shew you fweet Cæfar's wounds, poor, poor dumb
 mouths !
And bid them fpeak for me. But were I Brutus,
And Brutus Antony, there were an Antony
Would ruffle up your fpirits, and put a tongue
In every wound of Cæfar, that fhould move
The ftones of Rome to rife and mutiny.

    ALL.
We'll mutiny.———
    ANTONY.
Why, friends, you go to do you know not what.
Wherein hath Cæfar thus deferv'd your loves?
Alas! you know not. I muft not tell you then.
You have forgot the will I told you of.

    ALL.
Moft true,—the will.—Let's ftay, and hear the will.
    ANTONY.
Here is the will, and under Cæfar's feal.
To ev'ry Roman citizen he gives,
To ev'ry fev'ral man, fev'nty-five drachma's.

    2 PLEBEIAN.
Moft noble Cæfar !
    ANTONY.
Moreover, he hath left you all his walks,
His private arbours, and new-planted orchards,
On that fide Tiber ; he hath left them you,
         And

And to your heirs for ever ; common pleafures,
To walk abroad, and recreate yourfelves.
Heie was a Cæfar !

Is there any oration extant in which the
topics are more fkilfully felected for the
minds and temper of the perfons to whom
it is fpoken ? does it not by the moft gentle gradations arrive at the point to which
it was directed ? Antony firft fooths his
audience by affuring them, that Cæfar
loved the poor, and fympathized with their
diftreffes : by reminding them, that he had
rejected the proffered crown, he removes
from their fhallow underftandings all apprehenfion of that ambition in him which
the confpirators alledged as the motive of
their act : after thefe managements he proceeds further, and tells them of the will.
There is a delicate touch in the obferva-
tion, that Cæfar received the mortal
wound in the very mantle he wore the day
in which he had gained a victory over. the
Nervii, the fierceft of their Enemies. He
excites tender pity by mentioning the
ftab given. by his beloved Brutus. The
remark that he fell as a victim at the feet
of Pompey's ftatue, whom the lower fort
confidered as of a party unfavourable to
them, is another happy ftroke in this piece.

I am

I am forry that I muſt differ from the opinion of our commentator, who thinks the words, " O what a fall was there !" related to that circumſtance : it ſeems rather to refer to what immediately follows:

ANTONY.

Then I, and you, and all of us fell down :
Whilſt bloody treaſon flouriſh'd over us.

Meaning how the general ſtate of the republic was affected by the fall of ſo great a man As the illiterate people are afraid of being impoſed upon by the arts of the learned and the eloquent, he very judiciouſly aſſures them he is no orator. The refinements of the French theatre, perhaps, would not endure the mob of plebeians that appear in this ſcene. The fickle humour of the people, and the influence of eloquence upon their minds, are truly exhibited ; and I muſt own, as the imitation is ſo juſt, though the original may be called mean, I think it is not to be entirely condemned: one might perhaps wiſh the part of the mob had been ſhorter. The miſerable conceit of Cæſar's blood ruſhing out of the wound to aſk who ſo unkindly knocked, is indefenſible. The repetition of the words, honourable men, is perhaps too frequent.

The

The oration of Brutus, in many parts, is quaint and affected, an unhappy attempt, as the learned commentator obſerves, to imitate that brevity and ſimplicity of expreſſion, of which this noble Roman was a profeſſed admirer. Our author, who followed with great exactneſs every circumſtance mentioned in Plutarch, would probably have attempted to give to Antony the pomp of Aſiatic eloquence, if his good ſenſe had not informed him, that to be pathetic it is neceſſary to be ſimple.

The quarrel between Brutus and Caſſius does not by any means deſerve the ridicule thrown upon it by the French critic. The characters of the men are well ſuſtained; it is natural, it is intereſting; but it rather retards than brings forward the cataſtrophe, and is uſeful only in ſetting Brutus in a good light. A ſublime genius, in all its operations, ſacrifices little things to great, and parts to the whole. Modern criticiſm dwells on minute articles. The principal object of our poet was to intereſt the ſpectator for Brutus; to do this he was to ſhew that his temper was the furtheſt imaginable from any thing ferocious or ſanguinary, and by his behaviour to his wife, his friends, his ſervants, to demonſtrate,

ftrate, that out of refpect to public liberty, he made as difficult a conqueft over
his natural difpofition, as his great predeceffor had done for the like caufe over
natural affection.   Clemency and humanity add luftre to the greateft hero, but
here thefe fentiments determine the whole
character of the man, and the colour of
his deed.   The victories of Alexander,
Cæfar and Hannibal, whether their wars
were juft or unjuft, muft obtain for them
the laurel wreath, which is the ambition
of conquerors : but the act of Brutus in
killing Cæfar, was of fuch an ambiguous
kind,   as to receive its denomination from
the motive by which it was fuggefted ; it
is that which muft fix upon him the name
of patriot or affaffin.   Our author, therefore fhews great judgment in taking various opportunities to difplay the foftnefs and
gentlenefs of Brutus : the little circumftance of his forbearing to awaken the
fervant who was playing to him on the
lute, is very beautiful ; for one cannot conceive, that he whofe tender humanity re-
fpected the flumber of his boy Lucilius,
would from malice or cruelty, have cut
fhort the important and illuftrious courfe
of Cæfar's life.

Shakefpear

Shakefpear feems to have aimed at giving an exact reprefentation on the ftage, of all the events and characters comprehended in Plutarch's life of Marcus Brutus; and he has wonderfully executed his plan. One may perhaps wifh, that a writer, poffeffed of all the magic of poetical powers, had not fo fcrupuloufly confined himfelf within the limits of true hiftory. The regions of imagination, in which the poet is allowed an arbitrary fway, feem his proper dominion. There he reigns like Pluto over fhadows huge and terrible, of mighty and auguft appearance, but yielding and unrefifting. The terra firma of real life, and the open day-light of truth, forbid many pleafing delufions, and produce difficulties too ftubborn to yield to his art. On this folid foundation however our author knew he could always eftablifh a ftrong intereft for his piece.. Great knowledge of the human heart had informed him, how eafy it is to excite a fympathy with things believed real. He knew too, that curiofity is a ftrong appetite, and that every incident connected with a great event, and every particularity belonging to a great character, engages the fpectator. He wrote to pleafe an untaught people, guided wholly by their feelings, and to
thofe

thofe feelings he applied, and they are often touched by circumftances that have
not dignity and fplendor enough to pleafe
the eye accuftomed to the fpecious mira-
cles of oftentatious art, and the nice felec-
tion of refined judgment. If we blame
his making the tragic mufe too fubfervient
to the hiftorical, we muft at leaft allow it
to be much lefs hurtful to the effect of his
reprefentation upon the paffions, than the
liberties taken by many poets to reprefent
well-known characters and lights fo abfolutely different from whatfoever univerfal
fame, and the teftimony of ages, had
taught us to believe of them, that the mind
refifts the new impreffion attempted to be
made upon it. Shakefpear, perhaps not
injudicioufly, thought that it was more the
bufinefs of the dramatic writer to excite
fympathy than admiration; and that to acquire an empire over the paffions, it was
well worth while to relinquifh fome pretenfions to excellencies of lefs efficiency on
the ftage.

As it was Shakefpear's intention to make
Brutus his hero, he has given a difadvan-
tageous reprefentation of Cæfar, and thrown
an air of pride and infolence into his behaviour, which is intended to create an apprehenfion

prehenfion in the fpectator of his difpofition to tyrannize over his fellow-citizens.
In this haughty ftyle he anfwers the peti-
tion of Metellus Cimber, and the other
confpirators, for the repeal of Publius Cimber's banifhment : the fpeech fuits the
purpofe of the poet, but is very blameable
if compared with the hiftorical character
of the fpeaker, which ought certainly to
have been more attended to.   It will di-
vert the Englifh reader to fee what Mr. Voltaire affures us to be a faithful tranflation
of this fpeech ; and I will therefore give
the original and tranflation.   When Metellus is going to fall at Cæfar's feet, he
fays to him,

CÆSAR.

I muft prevent thee, Cimber.
Thefe crouchings and thefe lowly courtefies
Might fire the blood of ordinary men,
And turn pre-ordinance and firft decree
Into the law of children.   Be not fond,
To think that Cæfar bears fuch rebel blood,
That will be thaw'd from the true quality
With that which melteth fools ; I mean, fweet
          words,
Low-crooked curtfies, and bafe fpaniel-fawning.
Thy brother by decree is banifhed ;
If thou doft bend, and pray, and fawn for him,
I fpurn thee like a cur out of my way.
Know, Cæfar doth not wrong; nor without caufe
Will he be fatisfied

CÆSAR.

CÆSAR.

Cimber, je t'avertis que ces prosternemens,
Ces génuflexions, ces basses flateries,
Peuvent sur un cœur faible avoir quelque pouvoir,
Et changer quelquefois l'ordre éternel des choses
Dans l'esprit des enfans ; ne t'imagine pas
Que le sang de César puisse se fondre ainsi.
Les priéres, les cris, les vaines simagrées,
Les airs d'un chien couchant peuvent toucher un
    sot ;
Mais le cœur de Cæsar résiste à ces bassesses.
Par un juste décret ton frére est exilé.
Flate, prie à genoux, & léche moi les pieds ;
Va, je te rosserai comme un chien ; loin d'ici.
Lorsque Cæsar fait tort, il a toujours raison.

Ben Johnson, by a faulty transcript of
this speech, or the blunder of a player,
had been led into the mistake of charging
Shakespear with the absurdity of making
Cæsar say, he never did wrong without
just cause; and Mr. Voltaire has seized on
this false accusation.—It is perfectly apparent to any person who understands English, that Cæsar by preordinance and
first decree, means that ordinance and first
decree he had before past for Cimber's
banishment. And he says, I will not be
prevailed upon by these prostrations and
prayers of yours, to turn my decrees into
such momentary laws as children make.
If there had been any doubt of his meaning, the latter part would have cleared it.

CÆSAR.

Cæsar.

I was conftant, Cimber fhould be banifh'd ;
And conftant do remain to keep him fo.

It is furprifing that fome friend did not
prevent the critic from falling into fo
ftrange a blunder about changing the
eternal order in the minds of children.
Many of his countrymen underftand our
language very well, and could eafily have
explained to him the fignification of the
prepofition into, and that to change into
always fignifies to convert from one thing
to another. Sweet words, crooked curtfies, and bafe fawnings, he tranflates, the
airs of a fetting dog. *Lecher les pieds* is
not a proper tranflation of to fawn. Fawning courtiers would be ftrangely rendered
by feet-licking courtiers: a fawning ftyle,
a fawning addrefs, are common expreffions; but did any one ever think of a feet-
licking ftyle? a feet-licking addrefs? Nor
is *Je te rofferai* a jufter tranflation of I will
fpurn thee: the firft being a very low
phrafe; and to fpurn is in our language a
very noble one, and not unfit for the
higheft poetry or eloquence ; indeed is of-
tener fo ufed than in ordinary difcourfe,

Mr. Rowe in the Fair Penitent makes.
Horatio fay to Lothario,

I hold

I hold thee bafe enough
To break through law, and *fpurn at facred order.*

If Mr. Voltaire fhould tranflate thefe
words, he would triumph much that one
of our moft elegant poets talked of drub-
bing facred order. The tranflator feems
not even to know the Englifh alphabet;
for in tranflating Porcia's words,

PORCIA.
If it be no more,
Porcia is Brutus' harlot, not his wife.

He puts in a note upon Harlot, to affure us
that the word in the original is W————;
which if he underftood our blank verfe,
he would know could not make up the
metre.

Mr. Voltaire formerly underftood the
Englifh language tolerably well. His tranflation of part of Antony's fpeech to the
people, in his own play of the death of
Julius Cæfar, though far inferior to the
original, is pretty good ; and in his tragedy of Junius Brutus he has improved upon
the Brutus of our old poet Lee : he has followed the Englifh poet in making the daughter of Tarquin feduce the fon of Junius Brutus into a fcheme for the reftoration of her father; but with great judgment has imitated only what was worthy of imitation; and
by

by the ſtrength of his own genius has rendered his piece much more excellent than
that of Mr. Lee.

It muſt be allowed that Mr. Voltaire,
in his tranſlation of Shakeſpear, has nobly
emulated thoſe interpreters of Homer,
who, Mr. Pope tells us, miſunderſtand
the text, and then triumph in the auk-
wardneſs of their own tranſlations. To
ſhew he decides with the ſame judgment
and candour with which he tranſlates, it
will be neceſſary to preſent the ſentence
he has pronounced upon the genius of
our great poet. Speaking of Corneille
he ſays, he was unequal like Shakeſpear, and like him full of genius; *mais
le genie de Corneille etait à celui de
Shakeſpear, ce qu'un ſeigneur eſt à l'egard
d'un homme du peuple né avec le même
eſprit que lui.* I have given his own
words becauſe they do not carry any deter-
minate ſenſe. I conjecture they may be
thus tranſlated; The genius of Corneille
is to that of Shakeſpear, what a man of
great rank is to one of the lower ſort born
with the ſame talents of mind. When we
ſpeak of genius we always mean that
which is original and inherent, not any
thing produced or derived from what is
external.

external.   But Mr. Voltaire by faying the
genius of Corneille has that fuperiority
over our countryman, which a perfon of
rank has over a man in a low ftation, born
with the fame talents, perplexes the thing
very much.   It feems to carry the comparifon from the genius to the manner of the
writers.

If that manner is preferable, which gives
the moft becoming fentiments and the
nobleft character to the principal perfon of
his drama, there is no doubt but our poet
has perfectly eftablifhed his fuperiority
over his competitor; for it cannot be denied, that Cinna is *un homme du peuple*,
(a low fellow,) compared to Brutus.

Mr. Voltaire, in all the comparifons he
has made between thefe authors, has not
taken into the account that Shakefpear
has written the beft comedy in our language : that the fame man fhould have had
fuch variety of talents, as to have produced Macbeth and the Merry Wives of
Windfor, is aftonifhing.   Where is there
an inftance among the ancients or moderns
of one poet's uniting the fublime and pa
thetic, the boldeft inventions of fiction,
                                                 and

and the moſt juſt and accurate delineation
of characters; and alſo poſſeſſing the *vis
comica* in its higheſt perfection ?   The beſt
French poets have been thoſe

Who from the ancients like the ancients writ ;

and who have aſpired to the ſecondary
praiſe of good imitators : but all our critics allow Shakeſpear to be an original.
Mr. Pope confeſſes him to be more ſo than
even Homer himſelf.   It has been demon-
ſtrated with great ingenuity and candour,
that he was deſtitute of learning : the age
was rude and void of taſte : but what had
a ſtill more pernicious influence on his
works, was, that the court and the uni-
verſities, the ſtateſmen and ſcholars, affected a ſcientific jargon.   An obſcurity of
expreſſion was thought the veil of wiſdom
and knowledge; and that miſt common
to the eve and morn of literature, which
in fact proves it is not at its high meridian, was affectedly thrown over the writings, and even the diſcourſe of the learned, who often preferred images diſtorted
or magnified, to a ſimple expoſition of
their thoughts.   Shakeſpear is never more
worthy of the true critie's cenſure, than
in thoſe inſtances in which he complies
with this falſe pomp of manner.   It was

pardonable

pardonable in a man of his rank, not to be more polite and delicate than his cotemporaries; but we cannot fo eafily ex- cufe fuch fuperiority of talents for ftoop- ing to any affectation.

I may perhaps be charged with partia- lity to my author, for not having indulg- ed that malignant fpirit of criticifm which delights in expofing every blemifh. I have paffed over beauties and defects in the fame filence, where they have not effentially affected the great purpofes of the drama. They are of fo palpable a nature, the moft inattentive reader muft perceive them: the fplendor of his fine paffages is equally ftriking. It appears to me, that the dra- matic requires a different fpecies of criti- cifm from any other poetry. A drama is to be confidered in the light of a living body; regularity of features, grace of limbs, fmoothnefs and delicacy of com- plexion, cannot render it perfect, if it is not properly organized within, as well as beautiful in its external ftructure. Many a character in a play, like a handfome per- fon paralytic, is inert, feeble, and totally unfit for its duties and offices, fo that its

necefneceſſary exertions muſt be ſupplied by ſome ſubſtitute. The action is carried on much after the manner it is done in epic poetry, by the help of deſcription and narration, and a ſeries of detached parts.

It is unfair to judge ſingly of every line, in a work where the merit depends on the reſult of various operations, and repeated efforts to obtain a particular end. Works without genius are uſually regularly dull, and coldly correct, reſembling thoſe living characters that want, while

> They dream the blank of life along,
> Senſe to be right, and paſſion to be wrong *

Some allowances muſt be made to thoſe who are more animated and more employ-ed, if in the buſtle of great actions, and the exertion of great powers, they fall in-to ſome little errors. The genius of Shake-ſpear is ſo extenſive and profound, I have reaſon to fear a greater number of excel-lencies have eſcaped my diſcernment, than I have ſuffered faults to paſs without my animadverſion : but I hope this weak at-tempt to vindicate our great dramatic poet,

---

* Dr. Young's Satires.

M   will

will excite fome critic able to do him more
ample juftice.   In that confidence I have
left untouched many of his pieces, which
deferve the protection of more judicious
zeal and fkilful care.

F I N I S.